Endorsements for
Blue Like Jazz

"It's hard to find people who write about God from a position of commitment but still sound as if they're being human and honest, not running every word through the filter of religious subculture. Donald Miller is such a person. Plus, he writes with wit, flair, and self-awareness to boot."

—John Ortberg
Author of *Everybody's Normal
Till You Get To know Them*

"I can think of no better book than *Blue Like Jazz* to introduce Christian spirituality (a way of life) to people for whom Christianity (a system of beliefs) seems like a bad math problem or a traffic jam. Donald Miller writes like a good improv solo—smooth, sweet, surprising, uplifting, and full of soul and fury and joy. When I finished the last page, I felt warmed, full of hope, and confident that this great book will echo with beauty in many, many lives just as it is doing in mine."

—Brian McLaren
Pastor (www.crcc.org), author
of *A New Kind of Christian*,
and fellow in emergent
(www.emergentvillage.com)

"Donald Miller has achieved what every Christian writer toils and types for: spiritual relevancy. He has completely revealed himself in his latest effort. Laced with off-guard humor, biting insights, and to-the-point summaries, *Blue Like Jazz* is a thought-provoking journey toward a God who's not only real but reachable."

—David Allen
HM Magazine

"We need more people like Donald Miller, who are willing not only to interpret Scripture but the culture as well."

—**Ben Young**
Host of nationally syndicated radio show *The Single Connection* and coauthor of *The One* and *Devotions for Dating Couples*

"Honest, passionate, raw . . . real. Like jazz music, Donald Miller's book is a song birthed out of freedom. As with good music, *Blue Like Jazz* is more than true—it's meaningful. It's about Jesus, His story, and the freedom He longs to bring to you."

—**Paul Louis Metzger, Ph.D.**
Asst. Prof. of Christian Theology & Theology of Culture at Multnomah Biblical Seminary

"Donald Miller looks at faith the way a great jazz musician looks at a simple melody. He sees it as a thing to be explored, a passageway to a treasure trove of even richer melodies, rhythms, and harmonics. Thank you, Don, for daring to dig and explore. And thank you for sharing your wonderful discoveries."

—**Mark Atteberry**
Pastor and author of *The Samson Syndrome*

"Thank God for Jazz! With an improvisational mix of wry humor, soul-baring candor, and provoking commentary, Donald Miller composes a piece of literary and intellectual brilliance. Just like the music, you don't so much read *Blue Like Jazz* as you *feel* it—feel it and find yourself changed by its haunting melodic voice."

—**Julie Ann Barnhill**
National speaker, bestselling author of *Scandalous Grace*

Blue Like Jazz

Nonreligious Thoughts on Christian Spirituality

Donald Miller

THOMAS NELSON PUBLISHERS®
Nashville

A Division of Thomas Nelson, Inc.
www.ThomasNelson.com

Published in Nashville, Tennessee, by Thomas Nelson, Inc.

Published in association with the literary agency of Alive Communications, 7680 Goddard Street, Suite 200, Colorado Springs, CO 80920.

Library of Congress Cataloging-in-Publication Data

Miller, Don, 1971-
    Blue like jazz : nonreligious thoughts on Christian spirituality / Don Miller.
      p. cm.
    ISBN 0-7852-6370-5 (pbk.)
    1. Miller, Don, 1971- 2. Christian biography—United States. I. Title.
BR1725.M4465A3 2003
277.3'082'092—dc21   2003002223

Printed in the United States of America

06 07 08 09 RRD 23

For David Gentiles

Contents

Author's Note ix

1. Beginnings: God on a Dirt Road Walking Toward Me 1

2. Problems: What I Learned on Television 13

3. Magic: The Problem with Romeo 25

4. Shifts: Find a Penny 37

5. Faith: Penguin Sex 51

6. Redemption: The Sexy Carrots 59

7. Grace: The Beggars' Kingdom 79

8. gods: Our Tiny Invisible Friends 87

9. Change: New Starts at Ancient Faith 95

10. Belief: The Birth of Cool 103

11. Confession: Coming Out of the Closet 113

12. Church: How I Go Without Getting Angry 129

13. Romance: Meeting Girls Is Easy 139

14. Alone: Fifty-three Years in Space 151

15. Community: Living with Freaks 175

16. Money: Thoughts on Paying Rent 187

17. Worship: The Mystical Wonder 201

18. Love: How to Really Love Other People 207

19. Love: How to Really Love Yourself 223

20. Jesus: The Lines on His Face 233

Acknowledgments 241

About the Author 243

Author's Note

I NEVER LIKED JAZZ MUSIC BECAUSE JAZZ MUSIC doesn't resolve. But I was outside the Bagdad Theater in Portland one night when I saw a man playing the saxophone. I stood there for fifteen minutes, and he never opened his eyes.

After that I liked jazz music.

Sometimes you have to watch somebody love something before you can love it yourself. It is as if they are showing you the way.

I used to not like God because God didn't resolve. But that was before any of this happened.

In America, the first generation out of slavery invented jazz music. It is a free-form expression. It comes from the soul, and it is true.

Beginnings

God on a Dirt Road Walking Toward Me

I ONCE LISTENED TO AN INDIAN ON TELEVISION say that God was in the wind and the water, and I wondered at how beautiful that was because it meant you could swim in Him or have Him brush your face in a breeze. I am early in my story, but I believe I will stretch out into eternity, and in heaven I will reflect upon these early days, these days when it seemed God was down a dirt road, walking toward me. Years ago He was a swinging speck in the distance; now He is close enough I can hear His singing. Soon I will see the lines on His face.

My father left my home when I was young, so when I was introduced to the concept of God as Father I imagined Him as a stiff, oily man who wanted to move into our house and share a bed with my mother. I can only remember this as a frightful and threatening idea. We were a poor family who attended a wealthy church, so I imagined God as a man who had a lot of money and drove a big car. At church they told us we were children of God, but I knew God's family was better than mine, that He had a daughter who was a cheerleader and a son who played football. I was born with a small bladder so I wet the bed till I was ten and later developed a crush on the homecoming queen who was kind to me in a political sort of way, which is something she probably learned from her father, who was the president of a bank. And so from the beginning, the chasm that separated me from God was as deep as wealth and as wide as fashion.

In Houston, where I grew up, the only change in the weather came in late October when cold is sent down from Canada. Weathermen in Dallas would call weathermen in Houston so people knew to bring their plants in and watch after their dogs. The cold came down the interstate, tall and blue, and made reflections in the mirrored windows of large buildings, moving over the Gulf of Mexico as if to prove that sky holds magnitude over water. In Houston, in October, everybody walks around with a certain energy as if they are going to be elected president the next day, as if they are going to get married.

In the winter it was easier for me to believe in God, and I suppose it had to do with new weather, with the color of leaves clinging to trees, with the smoke in the fireplaces of big houses in opulent neighborhoods where I would ride my bike. I half believed that if God lived in one of those neighborhoods, He would invite me in, make me a hot chocolate, and talk to me while His kids played Nintendo and stabbed dirty looks over their shoulders. I would ride around those neighborhoods until my nose froze, then back home where I closed myself off in my room, put on an Al Green record, and threw open the windows to feel the cold. I would stretch across my bed for hours and imagine life in a big house, visited by important friends who rode new bikes, whose fathers had expensive haircuts and were interviewed on the news.

I have been with my own father only three times, each visit happening in my childhood, each visit happening in cold weather. He was a basketball coach, and I do not know why he left my mother. I only know he was tall and handsome and smelled like beer; his collar smelled like beer, his hands like beer, and his coarse, unshaven face smelled like beer. I do not drink much beer myself, but the depth of the scent has never left me. My friend Tony the Beat Poet will be drinking a beer at Horse Brass Pub and the smell will send me to a pleasant place that exists only in recollections of childhood.

My father was a big man, I think, bigger than most, stalky and strong like a river at flood. On my second visit to my father I saw him throw a football across a gym, drilling the spiral into the opposite hoop where it shook the backboard. There was no action my father committed that I did not study as a work of wonder. I watched as he shaved and brushed his teeth and put on his socks and shoes in motions that were more muscle than grace, and I would stand at his bedroom door hoping he wouldn't notice my awkward stare. I looked purposely as he opened a beer, the tiny can hiding itself in his big hand, the foam of it spilling over the can, his red lips slurping the excess, his tongue taking the taste from his mustache. He was a brilliant machine of a thing.

When my sister and I visited my father we would eat from the grill every night, which is something we never did with my mother. My father would crumble Ritz crackers into the meat and add salt and sauces, and I thought, perhaps, he was some sort of chef, some sort of person who ought to write books about cooking meat. Later he would take my sister and me to the grocery store and buy us a toy, any toy we wanted. We'd pace the long aisle of shiny prizes, the trucks and Barbies and pistols and games. In the checkout line I'd cling to the shiny, slick box in stillness and silence. On the drive home we'd take turns sitting on his lap so we could drive, and whoever wasn't steering would work the shifter, and whoever worked the steering wheel could drink from my father's can of beer.

3

It is not possible to admire a person more than I admired that man. I know, from the three visits I made to him, the blended composite of love and fear that exists only in a boy's notion of his father.

There were years between his calls. My mother would answer the phone, and I knew by the way she stood silently in the kitchen that it was him. A few days later he would come for a visit, always changed in the showing of his age—the new wrinkles, the grayed hair, and thick skin around his eyes—and within days we would go to his apartment for the weekend. About the time I entered middle school, he disappeared completely.

o   o   o

Today I wonder why it is God refers to Himself as "Father" at all. This, to me, in light of the earthly representation of the role, seems a marketing mistake. Why would God want to call Himself Father when so many fathers abandon their children?

As a child, the title *Father God* offered an ambiguous haze with which to interact. I understood what a father did as well as I understood the task of a shepherd. All the vocabulary about God seemed to come from ancient history, before video games, Palm Pilots, and the Internet.

If you would have asked me, I suppose I would have told you there was a God, but I could not have formulated a specific definition based on my personal experience. Perhaps it was because my Sunday school classes did much to help us memorize commandments and little to teach us who God was and how to relate to Him, or perhaps it was because they did and I wasn't listening. Nevertheless, my impersonal God served me fine as I had no need of the real thing. I needed no deity to reach out of heaven and wipe my nose, so none of it actually mattered. If God was on a dirt road walking toward me, He was on the other side of a hill, and I hadn't begun to look for Him anyway.

o   o   o

I started to sin about the time I turned ten. I believe it was ten, although it could have been earlier, but ten is about the age a boy starts to sin, so I am sure it was in there somewhere. Girls begin to sin when they are twenty-three or something, but they do life much softer by their very nature and so need less of a run at things.

I sinned only in bits at first—small lies, little inconsistencies to teachers about homework and that sort of thing. I learned the craft well, never looking my teacher in the eye, always speaking quickly, from the diaphragm, never feeble about the business of deception.

"Where is your homework?" my teacher would ask.

"I lost it."

"You lost it yesterday. You lost it last week."

"I am terrible about losing things. I need to learn." (Always be self-deprecating.)

"What am I going to do with you, Donald?"

"I am grateful for your patience." (Always be grateful.)

"I should call your mother."

"She's deaf. Boating accident. Piranha." (Always be dramatic. Use hand gestures.)

I also used a great deal of cusswords. Not those churchly cuss-words—*dang* and *darnit, dagnabit* and *frickin'*—but big, robust cusswords like the ones they use in PG movies, the ones the guys would say only to each other. Cusswords are pure ecstasy when you are twelve, buzzing in the mouth like a battery on the tongue. My best friend at the time, Roy, and I would walk home from school, stopping at the playground by the Methodist church to cuss out Travis Massie and his big sister Patty. Travis always made fun of Roy because his last name was Niswanger. It took me two years to understand why the name Niswanger was so funny.

Words turned to fists by the end of the year, and I was thirteen when I took my first punch. Square in the face. It was Tim Mitchell, the little blond kid who went to my church, and the whole time we were circling each other he was saying he was going to give me a fat lip, and I was shouting cusswords in incomplete sentences; scary cusswords. He hit me in the face and I went down beneath a sky as bright and blue as jazz music, and there were children laughing, and Patty Massie was pointing her finger, and Roy was embarrassed. There was a lot of yelling after that, and Tim backed down when Roy said he was going to give Tim a fat lip. Travis was singing the whole time: "nice-wanger, nice-wanger, nice-wanger."

Before any of this happened, though, when I was in kindergarten, I got sent to the principal's office for looking up a girl's dress during nap time, which is something that I probably did, but not for the immediately considered motive. It's more likely that her open skirt was in the way of something I really wanted to look at, because I remember the age quite well and had no interest whatsoever in what might be up a girl's dress. I received a huge lecture on the importance of being a gentleman from Mr. Golden, who stood just taller than his desk and had a finger that wagged like the tail of a dog and a tie with a knot as big as a tumor, and he might as well have been talking to me about physics or politics because I wasn't interested in whatever it was that I wasn't supposed to be interested in. But everything changed in the summer of my twelfth year.

Across the street from Roy's house was a large, empty field divided by railroad tracks, and it was there that I first identified with the Adam spoken of at the beginning of the Bible, because it was there that I saw my first naked woman. We were playing with our bikes when Roy stumbled across a magazine whose pages were gaudily dressed in colorful type and the stuff of bad advertising. Roy approached the magazine with a stick, and I stood behind him as he flipped the pages from the distance of a twig. We had found a portal, it seemed, into a world of magic and wonder, where creatures exist in the purest form of beauty. I say we found a portal, but it was something more than that; it was as if we were being led *through* a portal because I sensed in my chest, in the pace of my heart, that I was having an adventure. I felt the way a robber might feel when he draws a gun inside a bank.

At last Roy confronted the magazine by hand, slowly devouring its pages, handing it to me after diving deeper into the woods, off the trail common to us and our bikes. We were not speaking, only turning the pages, addressing the miraculous forms, the beauty that has not been matched in all mountains and rivers. I felt that I was being shown a secret, a secret that everybody in the world had always known and had kept from me. We were there for hours until the sun set, at which time we hid our treasure beneath logs and branches, each swearing to the other that we would tell no one of our find.

That night in bed, my mind played the images over as a movie, and I felt the nervous energy of a river furling through my lower intestines, ebbing in tides against the gray matter of my mind, delivering me into a sort of ecstasy from which I felt I would never return. This new information seemed to give grass its green and sky its blue and now, before I had requested a reason to live, one had been delivered: naked women.

o   o   o

All this gave way to my first encounter with guilt, which is still something entirely inscrutable to me, as if aliens were sending transmissions from another planet, telling me there is a right and wrong in the universe. And it wasn't only sexual sin that brought about feelings of guilt, it was lies and mean thoughts and throwing rocks at cars with Roy. My life had become something to hide; there were secrets in it. My thoughts were private thoughts, my lies were barriers that protected my thoughts, my sharp tongue a weapon to protect the ugly me. I would lock myself in my room, isolating myself from my sister and my mother, not often to do any sort of sinning, but simply because I had become a creature of odd secrecy. This is where my early ideas about religion came into play.

The ideas I learned in Sunday school, the ideas about sin and how we shouldn't sin, kept bugging me. I felt as though I needed to redeem myself, the way a kid feels when he finally decides to clean his room. My carnal thinking had made a mess of my head, and I felt as though I were standing in the doorway of my mind, wondering where to begin, how to organize my thoughts so they weren't so out of control.

That's when I realized that religion might be able to hose things down, get me back to normal so I could have fun without feeling guilty or something. I just didn't want to have to think about this guilt crap anymore.

For me, however, there was a mental wall between religion and God. I could walk around inside religion and never, on any sort of emotional level, understand that God was a person, an actual Being with thoughts and feelings and that sort of thing. To me, God was more of an idea. It was something like a slot machine, a set of spinning images that dolled out rewards based on behavior and, perhaps, chance.

The slot-machine God provided a relief for the pinging guilt and a sense of hope that my life would get organized toward a purpose. I was too dumb to test the merit of the slot machine idea. I simply began to pray for forgiveness, thinking the cherries might line up and the light atop the machine would flash, spilling shiny tokens of good fate. What I was doing was more in line with superstition than spirituality. But it worked. If something nice happened to me, I thought it was God, and if something nice didn't, I went back to the slot machine, knelt down in prayer, and pulled the lever a few more times. I liked this God very much because you hardly had to talk to it and it never talked back. But the fun never lasts.

My slot-machine God disintegrated on Christmas Eve when I was thirteen. I still think of that night as "the lifting of the haze," and it remains one of the few times I can categorically claim an interaction with God. Though I am half certain these interactions are routine, they simply don't feel as metaphysical as the happenings of that night. It was very simple, but it was one of those profound revelations that only God can induce. What happened was that I realized I was not alone in my own surroundings. I'm not talking about ghosts or angels or anything; I'm talking about other people. As silly as it sounds, I realized, late that night, that other people had feelings and fears and that my interactions with them actually meant something, that I could make them happy or sad in the way that I associated with them. Not only could I make them happy or sad, but I was responsible for the way I interacted with them. I suddenly felt responsible. I was supposed to make them happy. I was not supposed to make them sad. Like I said, it sounds simple, but when you really get it for the first time, it hits hard.

I was shell-shocked.

This is how the bomb fell: For my mother that year I had purchased a shabby Christmas gift—a book, the contents of which she would never be interested in. I had had a sum of money with which to buy presents, and the majority of it I used to buy fishing equipment, as Roy and I had started fishing in the creek behind Wal-Mart.

My extended family opens gifts on Christmas Eve, leaving the immediate family to open gifts the next morning, and so in my room that night were wonderful presents—toys, games, candy, and clothes—and as I lay in bed I counted and categorized them in the moonlight, the battery-operated toys of greatest importance, the underwear of no consequence at all.

So in the moonlight I drifted in and out of anxious sleep, and this is when it occurred to me that the gift I had purchased for my mother was bought with the petty change left after I had pleased myself. I realized I had set the happiness of my mother beyond my own material desires.

This was a different sort of guilt from anything I had previously experienced. It was a heavy guilt, not the sort of guilt that I could do anything about. It was a haunting feeling, the sort of sensation you get when you wonder whether you are two people, the other of which does things you can't explain, bad and terrible things.

The guilt was so heavy that I fell out of bed onto my knees and begged, not a slot-machine God, but a living, feeling God, to stop the pain. I crawled out of my room and into the hallway by my mother's door and lay on my elbows and face for an hour or so, going sometimes into sleep, before finally the burden lifted and I was able to return to my room.

We opened the rest of our gifts the next morning, and I was pleased to receive what I did, but when my mother opened her silly book, I asked her forgiveness, saying how much I wished I had done more. She, of course, pretended to enjoy the gift, saying how she wanted to know about the subject.

I was still feeling terrible that evening when the family gathered for dinner around a table so full of food a kingdom could feast. I sat low in my chair, eye-level with the bowls of potatoes and corn, having my hair straightened by ten talking women, all happy the holiday had come to a close.

And while they ate and talked and chatted away another Christmas, I felt ashamed and wondered silently whether they knew they were eating with Hitler.

2

Problems

What I Learned on Television

SOME PEOPLE SKIP THROUGH LIFE; SOME PEOPLE are dragged through it. I sometimes wonder whether we are moving through time or time is moving through us. My brilliant friend Mitch says that light, unlike anything else in the universe, is not affected by time. Light, he says, exists outside of time. He tells me it has something to do with how fast it travels and that it is eternal, but it is still a mystery to physicists.

I say this only because time kept traveling through me. When I was young I thought I had forever to figure things out. I am talking about feeling like Hitler. But I didn't. I didn't have long to figure things out. I believe that the greatest trick of the devil is not to get us into some sort of evil but rather have us wasting time. This is why the devil tries so hard to get Christians to be religious. If he can sink a man's mind into habit, he will prevent his heart from engaging God. I was into habit. I grew up going to church, so I got used to hearing about God. He was like Uncle Harry or Aunt Sally except we didn't have pictures.

God never sent presents either. We had this dumpy house and

dumpy car, and I had zits. Looking back, I suppose God sent sunsets and forests and flowers, but what is that to a kid? The only thing I heard from God was what I heard on Christmas Eve, that story I told you, when God made me feel so guilty, and I didn't like that at all. I didn't feel like I knew God, and yet He was making me experience this conviction. I felt that the least He could have done was to come down and introduce Himself and explain these feelings of conviction in person.

If you don't love somebody, it gets annoying when they tell you what to do or what to feel. When you love them you get pleasure from their pleasure, and it makes it easy to serve. I didn't love God because I didn't know God.

Still, I knew, because of my own feelings, there was something wrong with me, and I knew it wasn't only me. I knew it was everybody. It was like a bacteria or a cancer or a trance. It wasn't on the skin; it was in the soul. It showed itself in loneliness, lust, anger, jealousy, and depression. It had people screwed up bad everywhere you went—at the store, at home, at church; it was ugly and deep. Lots of singers on the radio were singing about it, and cops had jobs because of it. It was as if we were broken, I thought, as if we were never supposed to feel these sticky emotions. It was as if we were cracked, couldn't love right, couldn't feel good things for very long without screwing it all up. We were like gasoline engines running on diesel. I was just a kid so I couldn't put words to it, but every kid feels it. (I am talking about the broken quality of life.) A kid will think there are monsters under his bed, or he will close himself in his room when his parents fight. From a very early age our souls are taught there is a comfort and a discomfort in the world, a good and bad if you will, a lovely and a frightening. There seemed to me to be too much frightening, and I didn't know why it existed.

I was recently reminded about all of this.

○　○　○

It started while I was watching television. I live with four other guys, pretty cool guys in a pretty cool house in Laurelhurst. I have this killer room upstairs. It is tucked away from everybody, sort of hidden through a door in the back of the upstairs den. The walls in my room are cedar, like something you'd find in a wood cabin. There is a birch tree so big and dignified outside my window that I often feel I am in its limbs. In the evening when it rains, the birch sounds like an audience giving a standing ovation. Sometimes when the tree is clapping I stand at the window and say thank you, thank you, as if I am Napoleon.

Along my wood-paneled walls are small, wood-paneled doors that open into attic space. I stuck a television inside one of these doors, and in the evenings I lie in bed and watch television. When you are a writer and a speaker, you aren't supposed to watch television. It's shallow. I feel guilty because for a long time I didn't allow myself a television, and I used to drop that fact in conversation to impress people. I thought it made me sound dignified. A couple of years ago, however, I visited a church in the suburbs, and there was this blowhard preacher talking about how television rots your brain. He said that when we are watching television our minds are working no harder than when we are sleeping. I thought that sounded heavenly. I bought one that afternoon.

So I've been watching *Nightline* with Ted Koppel lately. He isn't as smart as Ray Swarez but he tries, and that counts. He's been in the Congo, in Africa, and it has been terrible. I mean the show is fine, but the Congo isn't doing so well. More than 2.5 million people have been killed in the last three years. Each of eight tribes is at war with the other seven. Genocide. As the images moved across the screen I would lie in bed feeling so American and safe, as if the Congo were something in a book or a movie. It is nearly impossible for me to process the idea that such a place exists in the same world as Portland. I met with Tony the Beat Poet the other day at Horse Brass and told him about the stuff on *Nightline*.

"I knew that was taking place over there," Tony said. "But I didn't know it was that bad." I call Tony a beat poet because he is always wearing loose European shirts, the ones that lace up the chest with shoestring. His head is shaved, and he has a long soul patch that stretches a good inch beneath his chin. He isn't actually a poet.

"It's terrible," I told him. "Two and a half million people, dead. In one village they interviewed about fifty or so women. All of them had been raped, most of them numerous times."

Tony shook his head. "That is amazing. It is so difficult to even process how things like that can happen."

"I know. I can't get my mind around it. I keep wondering how people could do things like that."

"Do you think you could do something like that, Don?" Tony looked at me pretty seriously. I honestly couldn't believe he was asking the question.

"What are you talking about?" I asked.

"Are you capable of murder or rape or any of the stuff that is taking place over there?"

"No."

"So you are not capable of any of those things?" he asked again. He packed his pipe and looked at me to confirm my answer.

"No, I couldn't," I told him. "What are you getting at?"

"I just want to know what makes those guys over there any different from you and me. They are human. We are human. Why are we any better than them, you know?"

Tony had me on this one. If I answered his question by saying yes, I could commit those atrocities, that would make me evil, but if I answered no, it would suggest I believed I am better evolved than some of the men in the Congo. And then I would have some explaining to do.

"You believe we are capable of those things, don't you, Tony?"

He lit his pipe and breathed in until the tobacco glowed orange and let out a cloud of smoke. "I think so, Don. I don't know how else to answer the question."

"What you are really saying is that we have a sin nature, like the fundamentalist Christians say."

Tony took the pipe from his lips. "Pretty much, Don. It just explains a lot, you know."

"Actually," I told him reluctantly, "I have always agreed with the idea that we have a sin nature. I don't think it looks exactly like the fundamentalists say it does, 'cause I know so many people who do great things, but I do buy the idea we are flawed, that there is something in us that is broken. I think it is easier to do bad things than good things. And there is something in that basic fact, some little clue to the meaning of the universe."

"It's funny how little we think about it, isn't it?" Tony shook his head.

"It really is everywhere, isn't it?" By this we were talking about the flawed nature of our existence.

"Yeah," Tony started in. "Some friends were over at the house, and they have a kid, about four or five years old or something, and they were telling me all about child training. They said their kid had this slight problem telling them the truth about whether or not he had broken something or whether or not he had put away his toys, you know, things like that. So later I started wondering why we have to train kids at all. I wondered, you know, if I ever had a couple of kids and I trained one of them, taught him right from wrong, and the other I didn't train at all, I wonder which would be the better kid."

"The kid you teach right from wrong, of course," I told him.

"Of course, but that really should tell us something about the human condition. We have to be taught to be good. It doesn't come completely natural. In my mind, that's a flaw in the human condition."

"Here's one," I said, agreeing with him. "Why do we need cops?"

"We would have chaos without cops," Tony said matter of factly. "Just look at the countries with corrupt police. It's anarchy."

"Anarchy," I repeated.

"Anarchy!" Tony confirmed in sort of a laugh.

"Sometimes I think, you know, if there were not cops, I would be fine, and I probably would. I was taught right from wrong when I was a kid. But the truth is, I drive completely different when there is a cop behind me than when there isn't."

And what Tony and I were talking about is true. It is hard for us to admit we have a sin nature because we live in this system of checks and balances. If we get caught, we will be punished. But that doesn't make us good people; it only makes us subdued. Just think about the Congress and Senate and even the president. The genius of the American system is not freedom; the genius of the American system is checks and balances. Nobody gets all the power. Everybody is watching everybody else. It is as if the founding fathers knew, intrinsically, that the soul of man, unwatched, is perverse.

o   o   o

Earlier that afternoon, the afternoon I got together with Tony, my friend Andrew the Protester and I went downtown to protest a visit by the president. I felt that Bush was blindly supporting the World Bank and, to some degree, felt the administration was responsible for what was happening in Argentina. Andrew and I made signs and showed up a few hours early. Thousands of people had already gathered, most of them protesting our policy toward Iraq. Andrew and I took pictures of ourselves in front of the cops, loads of cops, all in riot gear like storm troopers from *Star Wars*.

Andrew's sign said "Stop America's Terroism"—he spelled *terrorism* wrong. I felt empowered in the sea of people, most of whom were also carrying signs and chanting against corporations who were making slaves of Third World labor; and the Republican Party, who gives those corporations so much power and freedom. I felt so far from my upbringing, from my narrow former self, the me who was taught the Republicans give a crap about the cause of Christ. I felt a long way from the pre-me, the pawn-Christian who was a Republican because my family was Republican, not because I had prayed and asked God to enlighten me about issues concerning the entire world rather than just America.

When the president finally showed, things got heated. The police mounted horses and charged them into the crowd to push us back. We shouted, in unison, that a horse is not a weapon, but they didn't listen. The president's limo turned the corner so quickly I thought he might come tumbling out, and his car was followed by a caravan of shiny black vans and Suburbans. They shuttled him around to a back door where we watched through a chain-link fence as he stepped out of his limousine, shook hands with dignitaries, and entered the building amid a swarm of secret service agents. I was holding my sign very high in case he looked our way.

The president gave his speech inside the hotel and left through a side door, and they whisked him away before we could shake hands and explain our concerns. When we were done, I started wondering if we had accomplished anything. I started wondering whether we could actually change the world. I mean, of course we could—we could change our buying habits, elect socially conscious representatives and that sort of thing, but I honestly don't believe we will be solving the greater human conflict with our efforts. The problem is not a certain type of legislation or even a certain politician; the problem is the same that it has always been.

I am the problem.

I think every conscious person, every person who is awake to the functioning principles within his reality, has a moment where he stops blaming the problems in the world on group think, on humanity and authority, and starts to face himself. I hate this more than anything. This is the hardest principle within Christian spirituality for me to deal with. The problem is not out there; the problem is the needy beast of a thing that lives in my chest.

The thing I realized on the day we protested, on the day I had beers with Tony, was that it did me no good to protest America's responsibility in global poverty when I wasn't even giving money to my church, which has a terrific homeless ministry. I started feeling very much like a hypocrite.

More than my questions about the efficacy of social action were my questions about my own motives. Do I want social justice for the oppressed, or do I just want to be known as a socially active person? I spend 95 percent of my time thinking about myself anyway. I don't have to watch the evening news to see that the world is bad, I only have to look at myself. I am not browbeating myself here; I am only saying that true change, true life-giving, God-honoring change would have to start with the individual. I was the very problem I had been protesting. I wanted to make a sign that read "I AM THE PROBLEM!"

That night, after Tony and I talked, I rode my motorcycle up to Mount Tabor, this dormant volcano just east of the Hawthorne District. There is a place near the top where you can sit and look at the city at night, smoldering like coals and ashes beneath the evergreens, laid out like jewels under the moon. It is really something beautiful. I went there to try to get my head around this idea, this idea that the problem in the universe lives within me. I can't think of anything more progressive than the embrace of this fundamental idea.

o   o   o

There is a poem by the literary critic C. S. Lewis that is more or less a confession. The first time I read it I identified so strongly with his sentiments, I felt as though somebody were calling my name. I always come back to this poem when I think soberly about my faith, about the general precepts of Christian spirituality, the beautiful precepts that indicate we are flawed, all of us are flawed, the corrupt politician and the pious Sunday school teacher. In the poem C. S. Lewis faces himself. He addresses his own depravity with a soulful sort of bravery:

> All this is flashy rhetoric about loving you.
> I never had a selfless thought since I was born.
> I am mercenary and self-seeking through and through;
> I want God, you, all friends, merely to serve my turn.
>
> Peace, reassurance, pleasure, are the goals I seek,
> I cannot crawl one inch outside my proper skin;
> I talk of love—a scholar's parrot may talk Greek—
> But, self-imprisoned, always end where I begin.

I sat there above the city wondering if I was like the parrot in Lewis's poem, swinging in my cage, reciting Homer, all the while having no idea what I was saying. I talk about love, forgiveness,

21

social justice; I rage against American materialism in the name of altruism, but have I even controlled my own heart? The over-whelming majority of time I spend thinking about myself, pleasing myself, reassuring myself, and when I am done there is nothing to spare for the needy. Six billion people live in this world, and I can only muster thoughts for one. Me.

I know someone who has twice cheated on his wife, whom I don't know. He told me this over coffee because I was telling him how I thought, perhaps, man was broken; how for man, doing good and moral things was like swimming upstream. He wondered if God had mysteriously told me about his infidelity. He squirmed a bit and then spoke to me as if I were a priest. He confessed everything. I told him I was sorry, that it sounded terrible. And it did sound terrible. His body was convulsed in guilt and self-hatred. He said he would lie down next to his wife at night feeling walls of concrete between their hearts. He had secrets. She tries to love him, but he knows he doesn't deserve it. He cannot accept her affection because she is loving a man who doesn't exist. He plays a role. He says he is an actor in his own home.

Designed for good, my friend was sputtering and throwing smoke. The soul was not designed for this, I thought. We were supposed to be good, all of us. We were supposed to be good.

For a moment, sitting there above the city, I imagined life outside narcissism. I wondered how beautiful it might be to think of others as more important than myself. I wondered at how peaceful it might be not to be pestered by that childish voice that wants for pleasure and attention. I wondered what it would be like not to live in a house of mirrors, everywhere I go being reminded of myself.

It began to rain that night on Mount Tabor. I rode my motorcycle home in the weather, which I hate doing because the streets are so slick. I got home white-knuckled and wet. My room was warm and inviting, as it always is with its wood panels and dignified birch outside the window.

I sat on my bed and looked out at my tree, which by this time was gathering rain in applause. I didn't feel much like Napoleon that night. I didn't like being reminded about how self-absorbed I was. I wanted to be over this, done with this. I didn't want to live in a broken world or a broken me. I wasn't trying to weasel out of anything, I just wasn't in the mood to be on earth that night. I get like that sometimes when it rains, or when I see certain sad movies. I put on the new Wilco album, turned it up and went into the bathroom to wash my hands and face.

I know now, from experience, that the path to joy winds through this dark valley. I think every well-adjusted human being has dealt squarely with his or her own depravity. I realize this sounds very Christian, very fundamentalist and browbeating, but I want to tell you this part of what the Christians are saying is true. I think Jesus feels strongly about communicating the idea of our brokenness, and I think it is worth reflection. Nothing is going to change in the Congo until you and I figure out what is wrong with the person in the mirror.

Magic

The Problem with Romeo

WHEN I WAS A CHILD MY MOTHER TOOK ME TO see David Copperfield the magician. I think she had a crush on him. It was the same year he made the Statue of Liberty disappear on national television. Later he made a plane disappear and later still he got engaged to Claudia Schiffer.

David Copperfield said, at the beginning of the show, that there is no such thing as magic. Everything he would do would be an illusion. He got into a box and his sexy assistants turned the box upside down. When they opened it again he wasn't there. He made a lady levitate. He turned a tiger into a parrot, then back to a tiger, only the wrong color for a tiger, then back to the right color. Everybody gasped. There was a man in front of me with a fat head, so I had to lean over to see.

Later I became a magician myself. My mother bought me a magic set, and I studied the book that came with it. I could make three pieces of string turn into one long piece and one long piece into three pieces. I made a nickel pass through a plate. I guessed whatever card you pulled out of a deck. I was amazing. I was going to get very good at it, hire a sexy assistant and move to

Vegas. After a few months, though, I got frustrated because everything that was magic was only a trick, meaning it wasn't really magic, it was an illusion. I decided to grow up and become an astronaut with a sexy assistant. I imagined myself in a fancy white astronaut outfit with a girl who looks like Katie Couric gazing sheeplike at me while I worked levers and buttons on our flying saucer. Every few minutes Katie would wipe my brow.

Everybody wants to be somebody fancy. Even if they're shy. I have one friend who is so shy she wets her pants if you look at her. She doesn't really wet her pants, but she practically does. She is very good-looking, too, but never goes out because she is so shy. If you didn't know her pretty well, you wouldn't think she wants to do anything but hide in a closet. You wouldn't think she wants to be anybody people look at, but she told me after I got to know her that she wanted to be an actress. After you get to know her you forget how shy she is, so I told her to go and be an actress; she certainly is good-looking enough to be an actress. But later I thought that might not be a good idea because she'd probably get up in front of people and start crying or something because she is so shy.

I never wanted to be an actor, but I always wanted to be a rock star. Even when I was a magician I wanted to be a rock star. When I was young I would listen to the radio and pretend I was the singer and thousands of people were in the audience, all the girls I knew in the front row. I would wave to them while I was singing, and they would scream like their heads were going to explode. I wanted to be a rock star, but I never wanted to be an actor.

o   o   o

I've been to a play. It was *Romeo and Juliet,* and I took a date. It was my first date ever. Even though I never wanted to act myself, taking a girl to a play was a good move. My date sat so close to me I could hear her nose breaths. She felt warm like sunlight and soft like she used special soap.

Even though it is a good move to take a girl to a play, I screwed it up.

There is a part in the play where Juliet, the main girl, is standing on a balcony and Romeo, the main guy, is hiding in the bushes below. It is pretty tense because Juliet is going on about how she likes Romeo, but she doesn't know Romeo is in the bushes. It was great at first. My date scrunched in so close I could feel the softness of her side, the smoothness of her arms wrapped around mine. I thought what the actors were saying was pretty mushy, but I would make noises every few minutes as if they had said something beautiful. When I did this my date would glance at me in wonder. It is a pretty good idea to make some noises when you are at a play.

My date was wrapped up in the whole love theme, but I wasn't buying it. I didn't let on, I just wasn't buying a lot of the crap they were saying. Juliet kept going on about how Romeo should deny his family, and Romeo was like, Duh, okay. Then Juliet told Romeo that he smelled like a rose. Duh, okay, he said.

And then the key lines, the lines on which I now know the play hinges:

> Romeo: Call me but love, and I'll be new baptiz'd;
> Henceforth I never will be Romeo.

Later in the play they accidentally kill themselves. It was not very believable but that is what happened. My date was crying. I was thinking they got what they deserved. It seemed stupid to me. I didn't understand everything they were talking about, but what I did understand I thought must have been written for girls. People really should put a limit on how much they give to emotion. When we were walking out my date clasped my hand, and even though I wasn't feeling very mushy I smiled at her. We ascended the aisle and made our way through the crowded lobby onto the steps of the playhouse. There were girls everywhere, all of them misty-eyed. Two girls in front of us were talking to each other. One of them threw her arms in the air and cried out, *I wish I could know love like Romeo and Juliet!*

I couldn't take it anymore. I whispered under my breath, *They're dead.*

I didn't think anybody heard me, but my date did. Two girls next to us heard me also, and they told the people next to them. One idiot guy repeated what I said and laughed, pointing at me. All the girls looked at me like I had just stepped on a cat. My date's body grew cold. She let go of my hand. She crossed her arms over her chest and walked a few feet in front of me all the way back to the truck. On the way home she hugged the far door so tightly I thought she was going to fall out. When we got to her house I asked her if she would like to go out again.

"I don't think so," she said.

"Why?"

"I don't think I could like you."

"Why?"

"I just don't."

"Can we kiss? I hear that helps a girl fall in love."

"You are evil," she said. "The Antichrist!"

She went into her house, shutting the door firmly on our relationship. I honestly never liked her in the first place. She was pretty and all, but I never liked her deeply. I was only a little sad about it.

My mother had given me her Texaco card for my date, so on the way home I stopped in for some Cheetos and donuts. I sat in the Texaco parking lot and thought about poor old Romeo, begging for love, running off with his woman, and then accidentally dying. Some dates go terrible, it's a fact. If you would have asked me then, I would have told you he was doomed from the beginning. I figured he was doomed because he believed in magic. He believed hooking up with Juliet would make him new, change his name, have him baptized and shiny.

Everybody wants to be fancy and new. Nobody wants to be themselves. I mean, maybe people want to be themselves, but they want to be different, with different clothes or shorter hair or less fat. It's a fact. If there was a guy who just liked being himself and didn't want to be anybody else, that guy would be the most different guy in the world and everybody would want to be him.

One night, when I was watching television, I saw an infomercial about a knife that could cut through a boot and remain sharp enough to slice a tomato. They called it the Miracle Blade. Another night I saw a cleanser made with orange juice that could get blood out of carpet. They said it worked like magic.

The whole idea of everybody wanting to be somebody new was an important insight in terms of liking God. God was selling something I wanted. Still, God was in the same boat as the guy selling the knives and Juliet promising to make Romeo new. Everybody exaggerates when they are selling something. Everybody says their product works like magic. At the time I understood God's offer as a magical proposition, which it is. But most magical propositions are just tricks. The older you get, the harder it is to believe in magic. The older you get, the more you understand there is no Wizard of Oz, just a schmuck behind a curtain. I pictured my pastor as a salesman or a magician, trying to trick the congregation into believing Jesus could make us new. And, honestly, I felt as though he was trying to convince himself, as though he only half believed what he was saying. It's not that Christian spirituality seemed like a complete con, it's just that it had some of those elements.

The message, however, was appealing to me. God said he would make me new. I can't pretend for a second I didn't want to be made new, that I didn't want to start again. I did.

○   ○   ○

There were aspects of Christian spirituality I liked and aspects I thought were humdrum. I wasn't sure what to do. I felt I needed to make a decision about what I believed. I wished I could have subscribed to aspects of Christianity but not the whole thing.

I'll explain.

I associated much of Christian doctrine with children's stories because I grew up in church. My Sunday school teachers had turned Bible narrative into children's fables. They talked about Noah and the ark because the story had animals in it. They failed to mention that this was when God massacred all of humanity.

It also confused me that some people would look at parts of the Bible but not the whole thing. They ignored a lot of obvious questions. I felt as if Christianity, as a religious system, was a product that kept falling apart, and whoever was selling it would hold the broken parts behind his back trying to divert every-body's attention.

The children's story stuff was the thing I felt Christians were holding behind their back. The Garden of Eden, the fall of man, was a pretty silly story, and Noah and the ark, all of that, that seemed pretty fairy-tale too.

It took me a while to realize that these stories, while often used with children, are not at all children's stories. I think the devil has tricked us into thinking so much of biblical theology is story fit for kids. How did we come to think the story of Noah's ark is appropriate for children? Can you imagine a children's book about Noah's ark complete with paintings of people gasping in gallons of water, mothers grasping their children while their bodies go flying down white-rapid rivers, the children's tiny heads being bashed against rocks or hung up in fallen trees? I don't think a children's book like that would sell many copies.

I couldn't give myself to Christianity because it was a religion for the intellectually naive. In order to believe Christianity, you either had to reduce enormous theological absurdities into children's stories or ignore them. The entire thing seemed very difficult for my intellect to embrace. Now none of this was quite defined; it was mostly taking place in my subconscious.

○   ○   ○

Help came from the most unlikely of sources. I was taking a literature course in college in which we were studying the elements of story: setting, conflict, climax, and resolution.

The odd thought occurred to me while I was studying that we didn't know where the elements of story come from. I mean, we might have a guy's name who thought of them, but we don't know why they exist. I started wondering why the heart and mind responded to this specific formula when it came to telling stories. So I broke it down. Setting: That was easy; every story has a setting. My setting is America, on earth. I understand setting because I experience setting. I am sitting in a room, in a house, I have other characters living in this house with me, that sort of thing. The reason my heart understood setting was because I experienced setting.

But then there was conflict. Every good story has conflict in it. Some conflict is internal, some is external, but if you want to write a novel that sells, you have to have conflict. We understand conflict because we experience conflict, right? But where does conflict come from? Why do we experience conflict in our lives? This helped me a great deal in accepting the idea of original sin and the birth of conflict. The rebellion against God explained why humans experienced conflict in their lives, and nobody knows of any explanation other than this. This last point was crucial. I felt like I was having an epiphany. Without the Christian explanation of original sin, the seemingly silly story about Adam and Eve and the tree of the knowledge of good and evil, there was no explanation of conflict. At all. Now some people process the account of original sin in the book of Genesis as metaphor, as symbolism for something else that happened; but whether you take it metaphorically or literally, this serves as an adequate explanation of the human struggle that every person experiences: loneliness, crying yourself to sleep at night, addiction, pride, war, and self-addiction. The heart responds to conflict within story, I began to think, because there is some great conflict in the universe with which we are interacting, even if it is only in the subconscious. If we were not experiencing some sort of conflict in our lives, our hearts would have no response to conflict in books or film. The idea of conflict, of having tension, suspense, or an enemy, would make no sense to us. But these things do make sense. We understand these elements because we experience them. As much as I did not want to admit it, Christian spirituality explained why.

And then the element of story known as climax. Every good story has a climax. Climax is where a point of decision determines the end of the story. Now this was starting to scare me a little bit. If the human heart uses the tools of reality to create elements of story, and the human heart responds to climax in the structure of story, this means that climax, or point of decision, could very well be something that exists in the universe. What I mean is that there is a decision the human heart needs to make. The elements of story began to parallel my under-standing of Christian spirituality. Christianity offered a decision, a climax. It also offered a good and a bad resolution. In part, our decisions were instrumental to the way our story turned out.

Now this was spooky because for thousands of years big-haired preachers have talked about the idea that we need to make a decision, to follow or reject Christ. They would offer these ideas as a sort of magical solution to the dilemma of life. I had always hated hearing about it because it seemed so entirely unfashionable a thing to believe, but it did explain things. Maybe these unfashionable ideas were pointing at something mystical and true. And, perhaps, I was judging the idea, not by its merit, but by the fashionable or unfashionable delivery of the message.

○   ○   ○

A long time ago I went to a concert with my friend Rebecca. Rebecca can sing better than anybody I've ever heard sing. I heard this folksinger was coming to town, and I thought she might like to see him because she was a singer too. The tickets were twenty bucks, which is a lot to pay if you're not on a date. Between songs, though, he told a story that helped me resolve some things about God. The story was about his friend who is a Navy SEAL. He told it like it was true, so I guess it was true, although it could have been a lie.

The folksinger said his friend was performing a covert opera-tion, freeing hostages from a building in some dark part of the world. His friend's team flew in by helicopter, made their way to the compound and stormed into the room where the hostages had been imprisoned for months. The room, the folksinger said, was filthy and dark. The hostages were curled up in a corner, terrified. When the SEALs entered the room, they heard the gasps of the hostages. They stood at the door and called to the prisoners, telling them they were Americans. The SEALs asked the hostages to follow them, but the hostages wouldn't. They sat there on the floor and hid their eyes in fear. They were not of healthy mind and didn't believe their rescuers were really Americans.

The SEALs stood there, not knowing what to do. They couldn't possibly carry everybody out. One of the SEALs, the folksinger's friend, got an idea. He put down his weapon, took off his helmet, and curled up tightly next to the other hostages, getting so close his body was touching some of theirs. He softened the look on his face and put his arms around them. He was trying to show them he was one of them. None of the prison guards would have done this. He stayed there for a little while until some of the hostages started to look at him, finally meeting his eyes. The Navy SEAL whispered that they were Americans and were there to rescue them. Will you follow us? he said. The hero stood to his feet and one of the hostages did the same, then another, until all of them were willing to go. The story ends with all the hostages safe on an American aircraft carrier.

I never liked it when the preachers said we had to follow Jesus. Sometimes they would make Him sound angry. But I liked the story the folksinger told. I liked the idea of Jesus becoming man, so that we would be able to trust Him, and I like that He healed people and loved them and cared deeply about how people were feeling.

When I understood that the decision to follow Jesus was very much like the decision the hostages had to make to follow their rescuer, I knew then that I needed to decide whether or not I would follow Him. The decision was simple once I asked myself, *Is Jesus the Son of God, are we being held captive in a world run by Satan, a world filled with brokenness, and do I believe Jesus can rescue me from this condition?*

If life had a climax, which it must in order for the element of climax to be mirrored in story, then Christian spirituality was offering a climax. It was offering a decision.

The last element of story is resolution. Christian spirituality offered a resolution, the resolution of forgiveness and a home in the afterlife. Again, it all sounded so very witless to me, but by this time I wanted desperately to believe it. It felt as though my soul were designed to live the story Christian spirituality was telling. I felt like my soul wanted to be forgiven. I wanted the resolution God was offering.

And there it was: setting, conflict, climax, and resolution. As silly as it seemed, it met the requirements of the heart and it matched the facts of reality. It felt more than true, it felt meaningful. I was starting to believe I was a character in a greater story, which is why the elements of story made sense in the first place.

The magical proposition of the gospel, once free from the clasps of fairy tale, was very adult to me, very gritty like something from Hemingway or Steinbeck, like something with copious amounts of sex and blood. Christian spirituality was not a children's story. It wasn't cute or neat. It was mystical and odd and clean, and it was reaching into dirty. There was wonder in it and enchantment.

Perhaps, I thought, Christian spirituality really was the difference between illusion and magic.

Shifts

Find a Penny

SOME OF THE CHRISTIANS IN PORTLAND TALK about Reed College as if it is hades. They say the students at Reed are pagans, heathens in heart. Reed was recently selected by the *Princeton Review* as the college where students are most likely to ignore God. It is true. It is a godless place, known for existential experimentation of all sorts. There are no rules at Reed, and many of the students there have issues with authority. Reed students, however, are also brilliant. Loren Pope, former education editor for the *New York Times*, calls Reed "the most intellectual college in the country." Reed receives more awards and fellowships, per capita, than any other American college and has entertained more than thirty Rhodes scholars.

For a time, my friend Ross and I got together once each week to talk about life and the Old Testament. Ross used to teach Old Testament at a local seminary. Sometimes Ross would talk about his son, Michael, who was a student at Reed. During the year Ross and I were getting together to talk about the Old Testament, I had heard Michael was not doing well. Ross told me Michael had gotten his girlfriend pregnant and the girl was not allowing him to see the child. His son was pretty heartbroken about it.

During his senior year at Reed, Ross's son died by suicide. He jumped from a cliff on the Oregon coast.

After it happened, Ross was in terrible pain. The next time I got together with him, about a month after the tragedy, Ross sat across from me with blue cheeks and moist eyes. It was as if everything sorrowful in the world was pressing on his chest. To this day, I cannot imagine any greater pain than losing a child.

I never knew Michael, but everybody who did loved him. The students at Reed flooded his e-mail box with good-bye letters and notes of disbelief. Through the years after Michael's death, even after Ross and I stopped meeting because I moved across town, Reed remained in the back of my mind. Not too many years went by before I started thinking about going back to school. I wasn't sure what to study, but I heard Reed had a terrific humanities program. I am a terrible student. I always have been. Deadlines and tests do me in. I can't take the pressure. Tony the Beat Poet, however, told me he was considering auditing a humanities class at Reed: ancient Greek literature. He asked me if I wanted to join him.

At the time I was attending this large church in the suburbs. It was like going to church at the Gap. I don't know why I went there. I didn't fit. I had a few friends, though, very nice people, and when I told them I wanted to audit classes at Reed they looked at me as if I wanted to date Satan. One friend sat me down and told me all about the place, how they have a three-day festival at the end of the year in which they run around naked. She said some of the students probably use drugs. She told me God did not want me to attend Reed College.

o   o   o

The first day of school was exhilarating. It was better than high school. Reed had ashtrays, and everybody said cusswords.

There were four hundred freshmen in my humanities class. Dr. Peter Steinberger, the acting president, delivered a lecture of which I understood about 10 percent. But the 10 percent I understood was brilliant. I loved it. I made noises while he was teaching, humming noises, noises in agreement with his passionate decrees.

After class I would usually go to Commons to get coffee and organize my notes. It was in Commons where I met Laura, who, although she was an atheist, would teach me a great deal about God. Her father, whom she loved and admired dearly, was a Methodist minister in Atlanta, and yet she was the only one in her family who could not embrace the idea of God. She explained that her family loved her all the same, that there was no tension because of her resistance to faith. Laura and I started meeting every day after lecture, rehashing the day's themes. I don't believe I had ever met anybody as brilliant as Laura. She seemed to drink in the complicated themes of Greek literature as though they were cartoons.

"What did you think of the lecture?" I once asked her.

"I thought it was okay."

"Just okay?" I asked.

"Yeah, I mean, this is supposed to be a pretty challenging school, and I wasn't that challenged. Not that good of an introduction if you ask me. I hope they don't put the cookies on a lower shelf all year."

"Cookies?" I asked. I thought she had cookies.

Laura would go on to explain the ideas I didn't understand. In time she figured out that I was a Christian, but we didn't talk much about it. We normally discussed literature or the day's lecture, but one day Laura brought up an odd topic: racism in the history of the church. She had moved to Portland from Georgia where, though she is an atheist, she told me she witnessed, within a church, the sort of racial discrimination most of us thought ended fifty years ago. She asked me very seriously what I thought about the problem of racism in America and whether the church had been a harbor for that sort of hatred. It had been a long time since I'd thought about it, to be honest. Just out of high school I got hooked on Martin Luther King and read most of his books, but since then the issue had faded in my mind. I am sure there are exceptions, but for the most part I think evangelical churches failed pretty badly during the civil rights movement, as did nearly every other social institution. Laura looked down into her coffee and didn't say anything. I knew, from previous conversations, she had dated a black student back in Atlanta who was now at Morehouse College where Dr. King himself earned a degree. Her question was not philosophical. It was personal.

I told her how frustrating it is to be a Christian in America, and how frustrated I am with not only the church's failures concerning human rights, but also my personal failure to contribute to the solution. I wondered out loud, though, if there was a bigger issue, and I mistakenly made the callous comment that racism might be a minor problem compared to bigger trouble we have to deal with.

"Racism, not an issue?!" she questioned very sternly.

"Well, not that it's not an issue, only that it is a minor issue."

"How can you say that?" She sat back restlessly in her chair. "Don, it is an enormous problem."

I was doing a lot of backpedaling at first, but then I began to explain what I meant. "Yeah, I understand it is a terrible and painful problem, but in light of the whole picture, racism is a signal of something greater. There is a larger problem here than tension between ethnic groups."

"Unpack that statement," Laura said.

"I'm talking about self-absorption. If you think about it, the human race is pretty self-absorbed. Racism might be the symptom of a greater disease. What I mean is, as a human, I am flawed in that it is difficult for me to consider others before myself. It feels like I have to fight against this force, this current within me that, more often than not, wants to avoid serious issues and please myself, buy things for myself, feed myself, entertain myself, and all of that. All I'm saying is that if we, as a species, could fix our self-absorption, we could end a lot of pain in the world."

Laura didn't say much more that afternoon, but we got together several weeks later, and she hinted she agreed about this problem of self-absorption. She called it sin.

"Wait," I began. "How can you believe in sin but not in God?"

"I just do," she said.

"But you can't."

"I can do what I want." She looked at me sternly.

"Okay," I said, knowing that if we got into an argument she would win.

Laura and I didn't talk much about religion after that. She had dreams of becoming a writer, so we talked about literature. She would give me articles or essays she had written. I ate them. They were terrific. It was very much an honor to even know her. I could sense very deeply that God wanted a relationship with Laura. Ultimately, I believe that God loves and wants a relationship with every human being, but with Laura I could feel God's urgency. Laura, however, wanted little to do with it. She never brought up the idea of God, so I didn't either.

o o o

I felt alive at Reed. Reed is one of the few places on earth where a person can do just about anything they want. On one of my first visits to campus, the American flag had been taken down and replaced with a flag bearing the symbol for anarchy. As odd as it sounds, having grown up in the church, I fell in love with the campus. The students were brilliant and engaged. I was fed there, stimulated, and impassioned. I felt connected to the raging current of thoughts and ideas. And what's more, I had more significant spiritual experiences at Reed College than I ever had at church.

One of the things I cherished about Reed was that any time I stepped on campus I would find a conversation going about issues that mattered to me. Reed students love to dialogue. There are always groups of students discussing global concerns, exchanging ideas and views that might solve some of the world's problems. I was challenged by the students at Reed because they were on the front lines of so many battles for human rights. Some of them were fighting just to fight, but most of them weren't; most of them cared deeply about peace. Interacting with these guys showed me how shallow and self-centered my Christian faith had become. Many of the students hated the very idea of God, and yet they cared about people more than I did.

There were only a few students on campus who claimed to be Christians. Though I was only auditing classes, I was accepted into this small group. We would meet in the chapel to pray each week or hold Bible studies in one of the dorm rooms. It was very underground. Secret. There has always been a resistance to Christianity on the campus at Reed. The previous year, a few Christians made a small meditation room on campus on Easter Sunday. They simply turned down the lights in a room in the library, lit some candles, and let students know the room was there if anybody wanted to pray. When Easter morning rolled around, students decided to protest. They purchased a keg of beer, got drunk, and slaughtered a stuffed lamb inside the meditation room.

The perspective the students in our group had about the event was Christlike. They were hurt, somewhat offended, but mostly brokenhearted. The event was tough on our group. We did not feel welcome on campus. But I learned so much from the Christians at Reed. I learned that true love turns the other cheek, does not take a wrong into account, loves all people regardless of their indifference or hostility. The Christians at Reed seemed to me, well, revolutionary. I realize Christian beliefs are ancient, but I had never seen them applied so directly. The few Christians I met at Reed showed me that Christian spirituality was a reliable faith, both to the intellect and the spirit.

I knew that Laura would fit in with this group. I knew that Laura, no matter how far she was from God, could come to know him.

The story of how my friend Penny came to know God gave me hope for Laura. I was first introduced to Penny at a party on the front lawn, but I thought she was too good looking to talk to, so I sort of slid off into the crowd. Later she showed up at a prayer meeting we had in my friend Iven's room, and I got to know her pretty well. We discovered that we were both ridiculously insecure, and so we became friends. Penny is living proof that Jesus still pursues people. Even Reedies.

Penny had a crazy experience with God while she was studying in France. She gives all the credit to Nadine, another of the very few Christians at Reed, and a member of our little rebel religious outfit.

When Penny and Nadine first met, Penny wasn't a Christian. They had both spent their freshman years at Reed but never knew each other. Individually they decided to study at the same school in France during their sophomore year.

Penny wanted nothing to do with religion. Her perception of Christians was that they were narrow-minded people, politically conservative and hypocritical. Penny disliked Christians because it seemed on every humanitarian issue, she found herself directly opposing the opinions held by many evangelicals. She also felt that if Christianity were a person, that is all Christians lumped into one human being, that human being probably wouldn't like her.

After arriving in France, Penny was scheduled to spend a few weeks in Paris on vacation before heading north to Sarah Lawrence College in Rennes. When she arrived, she contacted some of the girls she would be studying with. One of these girls happened to be Nadine. You have to know that Penny and Nadine are very different, opposites in fact. It is amazing that they hit it off at all. Not only did they have completely different religious ideas, but they also came from starkly contrasting backgrounds. Nadine, for instance, descended from Scottish royalty, still having a copious amount of pomp in her bloodline. Penny was born in a green army tent on a hippie commune in the Pacific Northwest.

I should paint the background for you a little bit so you can understand why I find it so interesting these girls became friends: Nadine's grandmother was born into the Stuart clan, a royal family in Scotland. Her grandmother married and moved to the Congo where the family was stationed as diplomats for the Belgian government. Nadine's mother was raised with a slew of servants including a driver, a cook, a butler, and a nanny. She was never allowed to speak to her parents unless spoken to first. Nadine's mother ran her home in similar fashion, passing down many of the traditions of aristocracy.

When Nadine and Penny met in France it was as if they were exchanging notes from different planets. No less interesting than Nadine's story is Penny's, whose parents originally named her Plenty. She changed her name shortly after she realized she could. At the hippie commune where Penny was born, her parents experimented with drugs in an effort to find truth. The experiment failed, and her mother and father left the commune and moved to Florida where her father got a job working on boats.

Penny has painful memories of her mother slipping into delusion, first believing John Kennedy was her lover, then claiming she was being hunted by the FBI. Her mother was diagnosed as a paranoid schizophrenic when Penny was a child. Today Penny's mother lives on the streets of Seattle where she adamantly refuses help from anyone, including Penny.

Penny once told me that no matter how gingerly she put the puzzle of her past together, she was always cut by the sharp edges: the fact that her mother was stoned while giving birth, the enticing but deceptive delusions presented to her as a child, and the breakup, not only of her mother from her father, but her mother from all reality. When I talk to Penny about driving up to Seattle to meet her mother, she tells me that I wouldn't enjoy the experience, that her mother will hate me.

"She hates everybody, Don. She thinks people are out to get her. If I call her on the phone in the shelter, she will come to the phone and hang it up. She doesn't answer my letters. She probably doesn't even open them."

"But she was normal at one time, right?" I once asked.

"Yes, she was beautiful and fun. I loved my mom, Don, and I still do. But I hate that her mind has been taken. I hate that I can't have normal interaction with her."

When Penny was eleven her parents divorced, and after the breakup she moved west with her father, spending a year sailing around the Pacific on her father's sailboat before eventually settling in a tiny mountain town in eastern Washington.

During those first three weeks in France, it was comforting for Penny that Nadine cared so much about her past and her story. This helped Penny listen to Nadine's story, and one night while walking on a beach in the south of France, Nadine explained to Penny why she was a Christian. She said that she believed Christ was a revolutionary, a humanitarian of sorts, sent from God to a world that had broken itself. Penny was frustrated that Nadine was a Christian. She couldn't believe that a girl this kind and accepting could subscribe to the same religion that generated the Crusades, funded the Republicans, or fathered religious television. But over the year at Sarah Lawrence, Nadine's flavor of Christianity became increasingly intriguing to Penny. Penny began to wonder if Christianity, were it a person, might in fact like her. She began to wonder if she and Christianity might get along, if they might have things in common.

The first time Penny told me the story of how she became a Christian we were walking through Laurelhurst Park, the beautiful park down the street from my house where lesbians go to walk their dogs.

"Nadine and I would sit for hours in her room," she began. "Mostly we would talk about boys or school, but always, by the end of it, we talked about God. The thing I loved about Nadine was that I never felt like she was selling anything. She would talk about God as if she knew Him, as if she had talked to Him on the phone that day. She was never ashamed, which is the thing with some Christians I had encountered. They felt like they had to sell God, as if He were soap or a vacuum cleaner, and it's like they really weren't listening to me; they didn't care, they just wanted me to buy their product. I came to realize that I had judged all Christians on the personalities of a few. That was frightening for me, too, because it had been so easy just to dismiss Christians as nuts, but here was Nadine. I didn't have a category for her. To Nadine, God was a being with which she interacted, and even more, Don, Nadine believed that God liked her. I thought that was beautiful. And more than that, her faith was a spiritual thing that produced a humanitarianism that was convicting. I was really freaked out, because I wanted to be good, but I wasn't good, I was selfish, and Nadine, well, she was pretty good. I mean she wasn't selfish. So she asked me if I wanted to read through the book of Matthew with her, and in fact I did. I wanted to see if this whole Jesus thing was real. I still had serious issues with Jesus, though, only because I associated Him with Christianity, and there was no way I would ever call myself a Christian. But I figured I should see for myself. So I told her yes."

"So then you started reading the Bible?" I asked.

"Yes. We would eat chocolates and smoke cigarettes and read the Bible, which is the only way to do it, if you ask me. Don, the Bible is so good with chocolate. I always thought the Bible was more of a salad thing, you know, but it isn't. It is a chocolate thing. We started reading through Matthew, and I thought it was all very interesting, you know. And I found Jesus very disturbing, very straightforward. He wasn't diplomatic, and yet I felt like if I met Him, He would really like me. Don, I can't explain how freeing that was, to realize that if I met Jesus, He would like me. I never felt like that about some of the Christians on the radio. I always thought if I met those people they would yell at me. But it wasn't like that with Jesus. There were people He loved and people He got really mad at, and I kept identifying with the people He loved, which was really good, because they were all the broken people, you know, the kind of people who are tired of life and want to be done with it, or they are desperate people, people who are outcasts or pagans. There were others, regular people, but He didn't play favorites at all, which is miraculous in itself. That fact alone may have been the most supernatural thing He did. He didn't show partiality, which every human does."

"I never thought of it that way," I told her.

"He didn't show partiality at all, Don, and neither should we. But listen, this is the best part. We got to the part of the book where Jesus started talking about soil."

"Soil?"

"Yeah. There is a part in Matthew where Jesus talks about soil, and He is going to throw some seed on the soil and some of the seed is going to grow because the soil is good, and some of the seed isn't because it fell on rock or the soil that wasn't as good. And when I heard that, Don, everything in me leaped up, and I wanted so bad to be the good soil. That is all I wanted, to be the good soil! I was like, Jesus, please let me be the good soil!"

"So that is when you became a Christian!"

"No. That was later."

"So what happened next?" I asked.

"Well, later that month, it was in December, there was a raging party going on downstairs in the dorm, and I was pretty drunk and high, you know, and I wasn't feeling too well, so I started up the stairs to see if my friend Naomi was in her room, and she wasn't, so I went down to my room and sort of crashed on the floor. I just sort of lay there for a little while and then it happened. Now you have to promise to believe me."

"Promise what?"

Penny stopped walking and put her hands in her coat pockets.

"Okay, but I'm not crazy." She took a deep breath. "I heard God speak to me."

"Speak to you?" I questioned.

"Yes."

"What did He say?"

"He said, 'Penny, I have a better life for you, not only now, but forever.'" When Penny said this she put her hand over her mouth, as if that would stop her from crying.

"Really," I said. "God said that to you."

"Yes." Penny talked through her hand. "Do you believe me?"

"I guess."

"It doesn't matter whether you believe me or not." Penny started walking again. "That is what happened, Don. It was crazy.

God said it. I got really freaked out about it, you know. I thought maybe it was the drugs, but I knew at the same time it wasn't the drugs." Penny put her hand on her forehead and smiled, shaking her head. "I should read you my journal from that night. It was like, oh my God, God talked to me. I am having this trippy God thing right now. God is talking to me. I kept asking Him to say it again, but He wouldn't. I guess it's because I heard Him the first time, you know."

"Yeah, probably. So is that when you became a Christian, the night God talked to you?"

"No."

"You didn't become a Christian, even after God talked to you."

"No."

"Why?"

"I was drunk and high, Don. You should be sober when you make important decisions."

"That's a good point," I agreed. But I still thought she was crazy. "So what happened next?"

"Well," Penny started. "A couple of nights later I got on my knees and said I didn't want to be like this anymore. I wanted to be good, you know. I wanted God to help me care about other people because that's all I wanted to do, but I wasn't any good at it. I had already come to believe that Jesus was who He said He was, that Jesus was God. I don't know how I came to that conclusion. It wasn't like doing math; it was something entirely different, but I knew it, I knew inside that He was God. But this time I just prayed and asked God to forgive me. And that is when I became a Christian. It was pretty simple." Penny put her hands back in her pockets and looked at me with her gorgeous blue eyes. "There," she said. "Are you happy?" And with that last comment she stuck her tongue out and laughed.

"Tell me the story again, Penny. Start with arriving in France."

"Why?"

"Because it's a good story. Tell it again," I told her.

"No. Once is enough. You will probably put it in one of your Christian books or something."

"Never," I said adamantly.

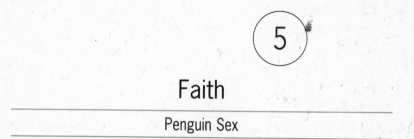

Faith

Penguin Sex

THE GOOFY THING ABOUT CHRISTIAN FAITH IS that you believe it and don't believe it at the same time. It isn't unlike having an imaginary friend. I believe in Jesus; I believe He is the Son of God, but every time I sit down to explain this to somebody I feel like a palm reader, like somebody who works at a circus or a kid who is always making things up or somebody at a Star Trek convention who hasn't figured out the show isn't real.

Until.

When one of my friends becomes a Christian, which happens about every ten years because I am such a sheep about sharing my faith, the experience is euphoric. I see in their eyes the trueness of the story.

Everybody at Reed was telling me something was wrong with Laura. They said she was depressed or something. I ran into her at a lecture in Vollum Lounge, which is beautiful like a museum with its tall white walls. Laura sat in front of me, and when the lecture was over she didn't leave. Neither did I. I didn't want to bother her, but I could tell she was sad about something.

"How are you?" I asked.

"I am not good." She turned to face me. I could see in her eyes she had spent the morning crying.

"What is wrong?"

"Everything."

"Boy stuff?" I asked.

"No."

"School stuff?" I asked.

"No."

"God stuff?"

Laura just looked at me. Her eyes were sore and moist. "I guess so, Don. I don't know."

"Can you explain any of it? The way you feel."

"I feel like my life is a mess. I can't explain it. It's just a mess."

"I see," I said.

"Don, I just want to confess. I have done terrible things. Can I confess to you?"

"I don't think confessing to me is going to do you any good." As I said it Laura wiped her eyes with her fingers.

"I feel like He is after me, Don."

"Who is after you?" I asked.

"God."

"I think that is very beautiful, Laura. And I believe you. I believe God wants you."

"I feel like He is after me," she repeated.

"What do you think He wants?"

"I don't know. I can't do this, Don. You don't understand. I can't do this."

"Can't do what, Laura?"

"Be a Christian."

"Why can't you be a Christian?"

Laura didn't say anything. She just looked at me and rolled her tired eyes. She dropped her hands into her lap with a sigh. "I wish I could read you my journal," she said, looking blankly at the wall. "There is this part of me that wants to believe. I wrote about it in my journal. My family believes, Don. I feel as though I need to believe. Like I am going to die if I don't believe. But it is all so stupid. So completely stupid."

"Laura, why is it that you hang out with the Christians on campus?"

"I don't know. I guess I am just curious." She wiped her eye again. "You're not dumb, I don't think. I just don't understand how you can believe this stuff."

"I don't either, really," I told her. "But I believe in God, Laura. There is something inside me that causes me to believe. And now I believe God is after you, that God wants you to believe too."

"What do you mean?" she asked, dropping her hands in her lap and sighing once again.

"I mean the idea that you want to confess. I think that God is wanting a relationship with you and that starts by confessing directly to Him. He is offering forgiveness."

"You are not making this easy, Don. I don't exactly believe I need a God to forgive me of anything."

"I know. But that is what I believe is happening. Perhaps you can see it as an act of social justice. The entire world is falling apart because nobody will admit they are wrong. But by asking God to forgive you, you are willing to own your own crap."

Laura sat silent for a while. She sort of mumbled under her breath. "I can't, Don. It isn't a decision. It isn't something you decide."

"What do you mean?"

"I can't get there. I can't just say it without meaning it." She was getting very frustrated. "I can't do it. It would be like, say, trying to fall in love with somebody, or trying to convince yourself that your favorite food is pancakes. You don't decide those things, they just happen to you. If God is real, He needs to happen to me."

"That is true. But don't panic. It's okay. God brought you this far, Laura; He will bring you the rest of the way. It may take time."

"But this hurts," she said. "I want to believe, but I can't. I hate this!"

Laura went back to her room. The next day I got an e-mail from Penny saying she, too, had talked with Laura. Penny asked me to pray for her as Laura felt trapped. Penny said she was going to spend a great deal of time with her, really walking through her emotions.

o   o   o

I had no explanation for Laura. I don't think there is an explanation. My belief in Jesus did not seem rational or scientific, and yet there was nothing I could do to separate myself from this belief. I think Laura was looking for something rational, because she believed that all things that were true were rational. But that isn't the case. Love, for example, is a true emotion, but it is not rational. What I mean is, people actually feel it. I have been in love, plenty of people have been in love, yet love cannot be proved scientifically. Neither can beauty. Light cannot be proved scientifically, and yet we all believe in light and by light see all things. There are plenty of things that are true that don't make any sense. I think one of the problems Laura was having was that she wanted God to make sense. He doesn't. He will make no more sense to me than I will make sense to an ant.

o   o   o

Tony and I were talking about Laura at the Horse Brass the other day; we were talking about belief, what it takes to believe, and he asked me how I believed in God.

I felt silly trying to explain it, even though Tony is a Christian. I felt as if I were saying I believed in Peter Pan or the Tooth Fairy, and yet I don't believe in Peter Pan or the Tooth Fairy. I believe in God, and as I said before it feels so much more like something is causing me to believe than that I am stirring up belief. In fact, I would even say that when I started in faith I didn't want to believe; my intellect wanted to disbelieve, but my soul, that deeper instinct, could no more stop believing in God than Tony could, on a dime, stop being in love with his wife. There are things you choose to believe, and beliefs that choose you. This was one of the ones that chose me.

"You know what really helped me understand why I believe in Jesus, Tony?"

"What's that?"

"Penguins," I told him.

"Penguins?"

"Penguins," I clarified. "Do you know very much about penguins?"

"Nope." Tony smiled. "Tell me about penguins."

"I watched a nature show on OPB the other night about penguins. They travel in enormous groups, perhaps five hundred of them, and they swim north in the coldest of winter, so far north they hit ice. They look like cartoons, like something out of that movie *Fantasia*. All five hundred of them swim till they hit ice then they jump out of the water, one by one, and start sliding on their bellies. They sort of create ruts as they slide, and they follow each other in a line. They do this for days, I think."

"They slide on their bellies for days?" Tony asked.

"Days," I told him.

"Why?"

"I don't know," I confessed. "But after a while they stop sliding, and they get around in a big circle and start making noises. And what they are doing is looking for a mate. It's crazy. It's like a penguin nightclub or something—like a disco. They waddle around on the dance floor till they find a mate."

"Then what?" Tony asked, sort of laughing.

"Penguin sex," I said.

"Penguin sex?"

"Yes. Penguin sex. Right there on television. I felt like I was watching animal porn."

"What was it like?" he asked.

"Less than exciting," I told him. "Sort of a letdown."

"So what does penguins having sex have to do with belief in God?" Tony asked.

"Well, I am getting to that. But let me tell you what else they do. First, the females lay eggs. They do that standing up. The eggs fall down between their legs, which are about an inch or something long, and the females rest the eggs on their feet. Then, the males go over to the females and the females give the males the eggs. Then, and this is the cool part, the females leave. They travel for days back to the ocean and jump in and go fishing."

"The females just take off and leave the men with the eggs?" Tony asked.

"Yes. The males take care of the eggs. They sit on them. They have this little pocket between their legs where the egg goes. They gather around in an enormous circle to keep each other warm. The penguins on the inside of the circle very slowly move to the outside, and then back to the inside. They do this to take turns on the outside of the circle because it is really cold. They do this for an entire month."

"A month!"

"Yes. The males sit out there on the eggs for a month. They don't even eat. They just watch the eggs. Then the females come back, and right when they do, almost to the day, the eggs are hatched. The females somehow know, even though they have never had babies before, the exact day to go back to the males. And that is how baby penguins are made."

"Very interesting." Tony clapped for me. "So what is the analogy here?"

"I don't know, really. It's just that I identified with them. I know it sounds crazy, but as I watched I felt like I was one of those penguins. They have this radar inside them that told them when and where to go and none of it made any sense, but they show up on the very day their babies are being born, and the radar always turns out to be right. I have a radar inside me that says to believe in Jesus. Somehow, penguin radar leads them perfectly well. Maybe it isn't so foolish that I follow the radar that is inside of me."

Tony smiled at my answer. He lifted his glass of beer. "Here's to penguins," he said.

o   o   o

In his book *Orthodoxy*, G. K. Chesterton says chess players go crazy, not poets. I think he is right. You'd go crazy trying to explain penguins. It's best just to watch them and be entertained. I don't think you can explain how Christian faith works either. It is a mystery. And I love this about Christian spirituality. It cannot be explained, and yet it is beautiful and true. It is something you feel, and it comes from the soul.

o   o   o

I crawled out of bed a few days later and cracked open the Bible on my desk. I didn't feel like reading, honestly, so I turned on my computer and fidgeted with a Sim City town I had been working on. I checked my e-mail and noticed one from Laura.

She had sent it in the early hours of the morning. The subject read: *So, anyway, about all of that stuff* . . .

Dearest Friend Don,

I read through the book of Matthew this evening. I was up all night. I couldn't stop reading so I read through Mark. This Jesus of yours is either a madman or the Son of God. Somewhere in the middle of Mark I realized He was the Son of God. I suppose this makes me a Christian. I feel much better now. Come to campus tonight and let's get coffee.

Much love,
Laura

6

Redemption

The Sexy Carrots

LONG BEFORE I LANDED IN PORTLAND BUT
shortly after my own conversion to Christian spirituality, I experienced periods of affinity with God. I would lie on my bedroom floor, reading my Bible, going at the words for hours, all of them strong like arms wrapped tightly around my chest. It seemed as though the words were alive with minds and motions of their own, as though God were crawling thoughts inside my head for guidance, comfort, and strength.

For a while, I felt as though the world were a watch and God had lifted the lid so I could see the gears. The intricate rules of the sociospiritual landscape were something like a play to me, and I was delighted at every turn in the plot.

The truths of the Bible were magic, like messages from heaven, like codes, enchanting codes that offered power over life, a sort of power that turned sorrow to joy, hardship to challenge, and trial to opportunity. Nothing in my life was mundane. After I became a Christian, every aspect of human interaction had a fascinating appeal, and the intricate complexity of the natural landscape was remarkable in its perfection: the colors in the sky melding with the horizon, those south Texas sunsets burning distant clouds like flares, like fireworks, like angel wings starting flight.

God was no longer a slot machine but something of a Spirit that had the power to move men's souls. I seemed to have been provided answers to questions I had yet to ask, questions that God sensed or had even instilled in the lower reaches of my soul. The experience of becoming a Christian was delightful.

o   o   o

I don't think, however, there are many people who can stay happy for long periods of time. Joy is a temporal thing. Its brief capacity, as reference, gives it its pleasure. And so some of the magic I was feeling began to fade. It is like a man who gets a new saw for Christmas, on the first morning feeling its weight and wondering at its power, hardly thinking of it as a tool from which he will produce years of labor.

Early on, I made the mistake of wanting spiritual feelings to endure and remain romantic. Like a new couple expecting to always *feel* in love, I operated my faith thinking God and I were going to walk around smelling flowers. When this didn't happen, I became confused.

What was more frustrating than the loss of exhilaration was the return of my struggles with sin. I had become a Christian, so why did I still struggle with lust, greed, and envy? Why did I want to get drunk at parties or cheat on tests?

o   o   o

My best friends in high school were Dean Burkebile and Jason Holmes. Dean and Jason were both on the tennis team, and I was good enough as a practice partner, so we spent the majority of our hot Houston nights pounding the courts at the city park. We'd show up early in the afternoon and play till ten or eleven when the city shut down the lights, then we'd sit in the parking lot and drink beer, and Jason would smoke pot.

Dean's dad was a recovering alcoholic who had been sober for something like seven years. He was a handsome man, short, but he talked with a tongue swagger the way John Wayne talked in *True Grit*. Mr. Burkebile had amazing stories of his drinking days. He told us that he was driving drunk one night and blacked out at the wheel, steering his car directly into a parked police cruiser. I always looked up to Dean's dad, what with his drinking stories and tattoos and that sort of thing. He worked in a hospital now and drove a black Volvo. My family had a Buick. My mother never drove drunk. My father probably did, but I hadn't seen him in years.

When Dean and Jason and I would sit around in the parking lot, I felt earthy and real, like a guy out of a movie. They both came from wealthy families whose lives didn't revolve around church. I felt cool when I was with them, very sophisticated, as if I were going to play at Wimbledon the next week, sipping wine and signing autographs after the match.

Dean and I were serving as copresidents of the church youth group at the time. Dean never took any of it seriously. He took being president seriously but not the stuff about spirituality, not the stuff about metaphysical things taking place in your life. I'd try to get him to go to church camp, but he never wanted to. Camp was at the end of the summer, and it was too close to the school year, and if he went to camp, he'd feel convicted and it would take him a good two months to start drinking again, so he never went. One time, right after I got back from camp, Dean bought two cases of beer and had me stay over at his house. He said I had to get drunk to get over the initial guilt so I could have a good time at all the fall parties. I drank about a case all by myself. Dean and

I walked over to the city park and shot baskets under the moon, staggering and swearing because we could never hit the rim.

I didn't mind the drinking, mostly. Dean was about the best friend a guy could have. He really cared about people, I think, and so did Jason for that matter. They just liked to have a good time like anybody. With me, though, it was different. I really wanted to please God. I mean, I sort of wanted to please God. I felt like God had done something personal and real in my life. I also felt that I should probably try staying sober for a while, being copresident of the youth group and all.

One night while hanging out by the tennis courts, Jason pulled out a pretty-good-size bag of weed. Dean hardly smoked the stuff. He hated the taste and said it never got him high. I had never tried it, but that night Jason was pretty insistent on all of us giving it a go. I wasn't big on the idea. I had already had about five beers and was feeling pretty drunk. I had heard you shouldn't mix those things. Dean started packing Jason's pipe, and Jason got pretty excited, so I told him I'd take a hit.

To be honest, it didn't do anything for me. Anything good. Like I said, I was already pretty drunk, and the pot just put me over the edge. I got sick about five minutes into it. I felt like I was stuck in a suitcase at the bottom of a ship in the middle of a storm. Everything started sloshing around in my stomach. My hands and forehead began to sweat and my knees felt weak and yellow. I was poultry.

o   o   o

We walked back to Dean's house, and I lay down in his dog-smelling backyard. I slipped into seasick dreams of alligators and TBN talk show hosts. Jason came out and lay next to me and went on and on about what truth was, and did I think there was anybody out there. Jason had come to believe that truth was something imparted to you when you were high. Later he would go off to college. Friends of mine told me that he became known for waking up miles from campus, in his underwear, never knowing how he got there. On this night he was telling me about truth, about how it is something you know but you don't know you are knowing it. He was saying the key to the meaning of life is probably on other planets.

"Don. Don." He tried to get my attention.

"What, man?" I lay there, seasick.

"They could live on that one, man."

"Who, Jason?"

"Aliens, man."

As soon as one of the guys sobered up enough to drive, they took me home. I crawled through my bedroom window, stretched out on the floor, and waited for the ship to run aground.

I wondered, in that moment, about the conviction I had felt so many years before, the conviction about my mother's Christmas present. I figured all of this was God's fault. I thought that if God would make it so I felt convicted all the time, I would never sin. I would never get drunk or smoke pot.

I didn't feel worldly wise that night, rolling over on my stomach trying to hold down the vomit. I didn't feel like a guy after a tennis match at Wimbledon. I don't guess Mr. Burkebile was all that happy when he was drunk and wrecking police cars either. If he was happy he probably wouldn't have sobered up, and he probably wouldn't have to attend all those meetings. I think the things we want most in life, the things we think will set us free, are not the things we need. I wrote a children's story about this idea, but it's not really for children . . .

There once was a Rabbit
named Don Rabbit.

Don Rabbit went to
Stumptown Coffee every morning.

One Morning at Stumptown,
Don Rabbit saw Sexy Carrot.

And Don Rabbit decided
to chase Sexy Carrot.

But Sexy Carrot was very fast.

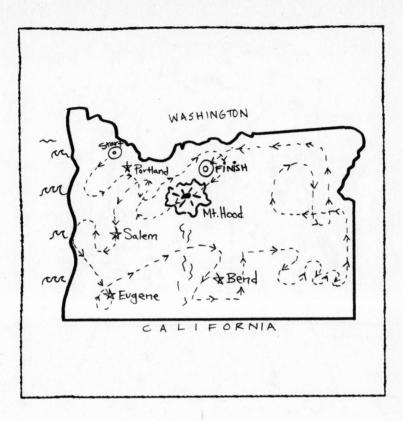

And Don Rabbit chased
Sexy Carrot all over Oregon.

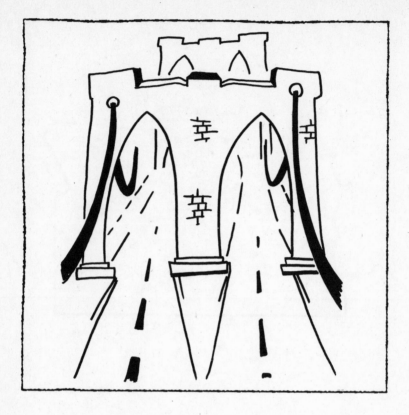

And all over America,
all the way to New York City.

And Don Rabbit chased Sexy Carrot
all the way to the Moon.

And Don Rabbit was very, very tired.

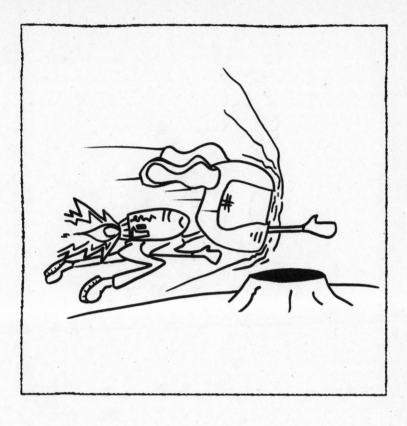

But with one last burst of strength,
Don Rabbit lunged at Sexy Carrot.

And Don Rabbit caught Sexy Carrot.

And the moral of the story is
that if you work hard, stay focused,
and never give up, you will eventually
get what you want in life.

Unfortunately, shortly after this story was told, Don Rabbit choked on the carrot and died. So the second moral of the story is:

Sometimes the things we want most in life are the things that will kill us.

And that's the tricky thing about life, really, that the things we want most will kill us. Tony the Beat Poet read me this ancient scripture recently that talked about loving either darkness or loving light, and how hard it is to love light and how easy it is to love darkness. I think that is true. Ultimately, we do what we love to do. I like to think that I do things for the right reasons, but I don't, I do things because I do or don't love doing them. Because of sin, because I am self-addicted, living in the wreckage of the fall, my body, my heart, and my affections are prone to love things that kill me. Tony says Jesus gives us the ability to love the things we should love, the things of Heaven. Tony says that when people who follow Jesus love the right things, they help create God's kingdom on earth, and that is something beautiful.

I found myself trying to love the right things without God's help, and it was impossible. I tried to go one week without thinking a negative thought about another human being, and I couldn't do it. Before I tried that experiment, I thought I was a nice person, but after trying it, I realized I thought bad things about people all day long, and that, like Tony says, my natural desire was to love darkness.

My answer to this dilemma was self-discipline. I figured I could just make myself do good things, think good thoughts about other people, but that was no easier than walking up to a complete stranger and falling in love with them. I could go through the motions for a while, but sooner or later my heart would testify to its true love: darkness. Then I would get up and try again. The cycle was dehumanizing.

Grace

The Beggars' Kingdom

I WAS A FUNDAMENTALIST CHRISTIAN ONCE. IT lasted a summer. I was in that same phase of trying to discipline myself to "behave" as if I loved light and not "behave" as if I loved darkness. I used to get really ticked about preachers who talked too much about grace, because they tempted me to not be disciplined. I figured what people needed was a kick in the butt, and if I failed at godliness it was because those around me weren't trying hard enough. I believed if word got out about grace, the whole church was going to turn into a brothel. I was a real jerk, I think.

I hit my self-righteous apex while working at a fundamentalist Christian camp in Colorado. I was living in a cabin in the Rockies with about seven other guys, and the whole lot of us fell into this militant Christianity that says you should live like a Navy SEAL for Jesus. I am absolutely ashamed to admit this now.

We would fast all the time, pray together twice each day, memorize Scripture, pat each other on the back and that sort of thing. Summer was coming to a close, and we were getting pretty proud of ourselves because we had read a great deal of

Scripture and hadn't gotten anybody pregnant. We were concerned, however, about what to do after we split up, thinking that if we didn't have each other we'd fall apart and start selling drugs to children. One of us, and it was probably me, decided to create a contract that listed things we wouldn't do for an entire year, like watch television or smoke pipes or listen to music. It was the constitution of our self-righteous individualism. The contract stated we would read the Bible every day, pray, and memorize certain long passages of Scripture. We sat around one night with pen and paper and offered sacrifices, each of us trying to outman the other with bigger and brighter lambs for the slaughter. We were the direct opposite of a frat house; instead of funneling our testosterone into binge drinking and rowdy parties, we were manning up to Jesus, bumping Him chest to chest as it were, like Bible salesmen on steroids.

I hitched a ride back to Oregon and got an apartment in the suburbs where I didn't know anybody and nobody knew me. I had this necklace on my neck, this string of beads, each bead representing one of the guys in the contract, and a cross in the center, a reminder that we had all gone in on this thing, that we were going to be monks for a year. At first it was easy, living in a new place and all, a new city, but after a while that necklace started to choke me.

The first of the exploits to go was the Bible. It wasn't that I didn't want to read it or didn't agree with it, I would just forget. It sat on the floor next to my bed beneath a pile of dirty clothes. Out of sight, out of mind. I'd forget about it for a month until I cleaned my room, and then I'd lift up a pile of dirty clothes and there would be my Bible, staring up at me like a dead pet.

One evening I was walking around Pioneer Square in downtown Portland when I noticed a pipe and tobacco store across the street. I decided I'd step inside and take a look-see. I came out with a new pipe that I swore I wouldn't smoke till the year was up.

It was a good deal, you know, about fifteen dollars or something. I couldn't pass up the sale on tobacco, either, even though it would go bad before the contract expired. I sat down in Pioneer Square with the skateboarders and musicians, chess players and coffee drinkers. I decided to pack my pipe, just to get a feel for it. I stuck it in my mouth to bring back that sensation, the feel of the stem between my teeth. Then I lit it. Then I smoked it.

After the Bible and the pipe thing fell apart, I decided to yield a bit on the television aspect of the contract. There was this indie pizza place down the street from my apartment, Escape from New York Pizza or something like that, and they had a big-screen television. I'd go down and watch Monday night football, which was a double sin because on Mondays we were supposed to be fasting. I figured none of the guys would mind if I switched the fasting day to Wednesday, just to shuffle things around. I shuffled so many fasting days around that after three months I was supposed to go twelve days without eating. I think I fasted twice that year. Maybe.

I hated the entire year. Hated it. I felt like a failure every morning. I hated looking in the mirror because I was a flop. I got ticked at all the people who were having fun with their lives.

I'd walk home from the pizza place feeling criminal for my mischief, feeling as though I were not cut out to be a Christian, wondering what my punishment would be for disobeying God. Everything was failing. I'd get letters from the other guys, too, some of them doing quite well. I wouldn't answer them. Not only was I failing God, I was failing my fundamentalist brothers!

o　　o　　o

My pastor, who is one of my best friends, experienced similar emotions early in his faith. Rick became a Christian when he was nineteen. Before he became a Christian he played football at Chico State, which, at the time, was the number one party school in the nation. And Rick did his share of partying. After months of drunken binges, though, he began to wonder whether there was anything more fulfilling in life than alcohol and sex. He began to long for God. So the next Sunday morning he made a point of being sober, and in fact walked to a local church to attend services. This was Rick's first time to step foot inside a church, and that morning the pastor happened to talk about sin, and how we are all sinners, and he talked about Jesus, and how Jesus died so that God could forgive us of our sin. At the end of the service, Rick prayed and became a Christian.

After a few weeks the pastors from Rick's new church came to visit, each in their suit and tie, and Rick entertained them and made them coffee, all of them sitting around sipping their coffee and talking nicely while the smell of marijuana lofted above their heads. Rick's friend was smoking pot in the next room. Rick laughs when he tells me he offered the pastors a hit, not being too offended when they turned him down.

The pastors talked to Rick about his conversion, explaining that he had been forgiven of his sins, and that it was important to try to live a righteous life. And Rick agreed with them, noting how much easier it would be to listen to the sermon on Sunday morning if he didn't have a hangover. So Rick began to choose purity over sin, and for a while he did well, but soon he found that he wanted to party with his friends, or he wanted to have sex with his girlfriend, and from time to time he would fail at his moral efforts. Rick tells me that those were the most depressing moments of his life, because he felt that he was failing the God who had saved him.

My pastor was anguished by an inability to control his desires. He felt that he had been given this new life, this key to heaven, and yet couldn't obey Jesus in return. So one evening he got on his knees and told God he was sorry. He told God how much he wished he could be good and obedient. He then sat on the edge of his bed and swallowed enough muscle relaxants and sleeping pills to kill three people. He lay down in a fetal position and waited to die.

o   o   o

Rick tells me, looking back, that he was too proud to receive free grace from God. He didn't know how to live within a system where nobody owes anybody else anything. And the harder it was for Rick to pay God back, the more he wanted to hide. God was his loan shark, so to speak. Though he understood that God wanted nothing in return, his mind could not communicate this fact to his heart, so his life was something like torture.

For a very long time, I could not understand why some people have no trouble accepting the grace of God while others experience immense difficulty. I counted myself as one of the ones who had trouble. I would hear about grace, read about grace, and even sing about grace, but accepting grace is an action I could not understand. It seemed wrong to me not to have to pay for my sin, not to feel guilty about it or kick myself around. More than that, grace did not seem like the thing I was looking for. It was too easy. I wanted to feel as though I earned my forgiveness, as though God and I were buddies doing favors for each other.

Enlightenment came in an unexpected place: a grocery store. I was on my way over Mount Hood to spend some time in the high desert with a few friends. I was driving alone and decided to stop in at Safeway to pick up some provisions for the weekend. While standing in line at the checkout counter, the lady in front of me pulled out food stamps to pay for her groceries. I had never seen food stamps before. They were more colorful than I imagined and looked more like money than stamps. It was obvious as she unfolded the currency that she, I, and the checkout girl were quite uncomfortable with the interaction. I wished there was something I could do. I wished I could pay for her groceries myself, but to do so would have been to cause a greater scene. The checkout girl quickly performed her job, signing and verifying a few documents, then filed the lady through the line. The woman never lifted her head as she organized her bags of groceries and set them into her cart. She walked away from the checkout stand in the sort of stiff movements a person uses when they know they are being watched.

On the drive over the mountain that afternoon, I realized that it was not the woman who should be pitied, it was me. Somehow I had come to believe that because a person is in need, they are candidates for sympathy, not just charity. It was not that I wanted to buy her groceries, the government was already doing that. I wanted to buy her dignity. And yet, by judging her, I was the one taking her dignity away.

I wonder what it would be like to use food stamps for a month. I wonder how that would feel, standing in line at the grocery store, pulling from my wallet the bright currency of poverty, feeling the probing eyes of the customers as they studied my clothes and the items in my cart: frozen pizza, name-brand milk, coffee. I would want to explain to them that I have a good job and make good money.

I love to give charity, but I don't want to be charity. This is why I have so much trouble with grace.

A few years ago I was listing prayer requests to a friend. As I listed my requests, I mentioned many of my friends and family but never spoke about my personal problems. My friend candidly asked me to reveal my own struggles, but I told him no, that my problems weren't that bad. My friend answered quickly, in the voice of a confident teacher, "Don, you are not above the charity of God." In that instant he revealed my motives were not noble, they were prideful. It wasn't that I cared about my friends more than myself, it was that I believed I was above the grace of God.

Like Rick, I am too prideful to accept the grace of God. It isn't that I want to earn my own way to give something to God, it's that I want to earn my own way so I won't be charity.

As I drove over the mountain that afternoon, realizing I was too proud to receive God's grace, I was humbled. Who am I to think myself above God's charity? And why would I forsake the riches of God's righteousness for the dung of my own ego?

o   o   o

Rick tells me that as he lay there in his bed waiting to die, he heard God say to him, "Your life is not your own, but you have been bought with a price," and at this point he felt a certain peace. Rick told me he understood, cognitively as well as emotionally, that his role in his relationship with God was to humbly receive God's unconditional love.

My pastor, of course, is still alive, a miracle he cannot explain. Before he could save himself, he drifted into sleep, but he woke the next morning with ample energy, as if he had never swallowed the pills at all.

After surviving the suicide attempt, Rick went to Bible college, married a girl he met in school, and now they have four children. A little over a year ago he planted a church in downtown Portland, widely considered the most unchurched region in the United States. There were only about eight of us at our first meeting, and now the church has grown to more than five hundred people. On a given Sunday there are dozens of nonbelievers at our church, and each week Rick shares with them the patient love of God. He talks about Jesus as if he knows Him, as if he has talked to Him on the phone earlier that morning. Rick loves God because he accepts God's unconditional love first.

Rick says that I will love God because he first loved me. I will obey God because I love God. But if I cannot accept God's love, I cannot love Him in return, and I cannot obey Him. Self-discipline will never make us feel righteous or clean; accepting God's love will. The ability to accept God's unconditional grace and ferocious love is all the fuel we need to obey Him in return. Accepting God's kindness and free love is something the devil does not want us to do. If we hear, in our inner ear, a voice saying we are failures, we are losers, we will never amount to anything, this is the voice of Satan trying to convince the bride that the groom does not love her. This is not the voice of God. God woos us with kindness, He changes our character with the passion of His love.

o   o   o

We dream of Christ's love for His bride reading like *Romeo and Juliet;* two equals enflamed in liberal love. I think it is more like Lucentio's pursuit of Bianca in *The Taming of the Shrew.* That is, the groom endearing the belligerent bride with kindness, patience, and love.

Our "behavior" will not be changed long with self-discipline, but fall in love and a human will accomplish what he never thought possible. The laziest of men will swim the English channel to win his woman. I think what Rick said is worth repeating that by accepting God's love for us, we fall in love with Him, and only then do we have the fuel we need to obey.

In exchange for our humility and willingness to accept the charity of God, we are given a kingdom. And a beggars's kingdom is better than a proud man's delusion.

8

gods

Our Tiny Invisible Friends

EVERY YEAR OR SO I START PONDERING AT HOW silly the whole God thing is. Every Christian knows they will deal with doubt. And they will. But when it comes it seems so very real and frightening, as if your entire universe is going to fall apart. I remember a specific time when I was laying there in bed thinking about the absurdity of my belief. *God. Who believes in God? It all seems so very silly.*

I felt as if believing in God was no more rational than having an imaginary friend. They have names for people who have imaginary friends, you know. They keep them in special hospitals. Maybe my faith in God was a form of insanity. Maybe I was losing my marbles. I start out believing in Christ, and the next thing you know I am having tea with the Easter Bunny or waltzing with my toaster, shouting, "The redcoats are coming!"

And then I started thinking about other religions. I wasn't seriously cheating on God or anything, I was just thinking about them. I read through the Koran before it was even popular. It never occurred to me that if Christianity was not rational, neither were other religions. There were times I wished

I was a Buddhist, that is, I wished I could believe that stuff was true, even though I didn't know exactly what a Buddhist believed. I wondered what it would be like to rub some fat guy's belly and suddenly be overtaken with good thoughts and disciplined actions and a new car. I would go into real estate and marry a beautiful blond, and when the beautiful blond tilted her head to the side as I talked about socialized education, I could rub the Buddha, and she would have the intellect of Susan Faludi. Or Katie Couric.

o   o   o

About the time I was thinking through some of this stuff, really letting my imagination go into creative answers about the meaning of the universe, I took the bus to Powells because one of my favorite authors was scheduled to read from his new book. Powells, I should tell you, is the largest bookstore in the world. New and used books. Cheap food, one of my friends says about it. Powells is one of the reasons I love Portland. The old downtown building houses more than a half million books, all of them smelling like dust and ink, two terrible smells that blend mystically to make something beautiful. Powells is another church to me, a paperback sort of heaven.

When an author speaks at Powells, I go early to browse. I start in the literature section and move to religion before glancing through politics and social movements, then finally to art, which is where they house author events. The writer I went to see that night is a Christian guy, a fisherman and outdoorsman who writes stories about fly-fishing and Oregon waters. All of the chairs were taken when I got there, so I was leaning against a pole when he entered the room. He was taller than I imagined, skinnier, with languid legs and arms. He wore khaki pants and a plaid flannel shirt. He looked like somebody who watches PBS, or like a man who knew a lot about birds.

The author came in through the back of the crowd, appearing from the stairwell, escorted by a Powells employee around the short shelf that held autographed copies of his books. He had newspapers in his hands and a file folder, papers disheveled within. He had a weathered copy of his newest book. He was introduced as one of Oregon's treasures, a great writer who brings water to life, giving us in his words the beauty of the out-doors and a reminder that we are human, having a beautiful experience. The audience applauded, and I let out a little hoot. The author gathered himself at the podium with a smile, gentle enough, and started the evening by reading from national news-paper articles on foreign policy and religion, leisurely flipping through editorials. He read as if he were sharing old family recipes, as if we were all taking notes, which we weren't.

He was having a bad night I think, or a bad year or some-thing, because he was a little sluggish and seemed to be reading from the articles as if to prove that other people agreed with his political ideas. We sat uncomfortably as he shared his opinion on one political idea after another, followed by a columnist who proved his idea. I really wanted him to read about fish. Fish are so safe, really. There is not a lot that is scandalous about fish. I began to turn on him to be honest. It was like watching Ernest Hemingway impersonate Ray Swarez.

The author I am talking about is a great writer. I want you to know that. I dearly love the man's work. And if he wants to read from the newspaper, who am I to tell him he can't? If he wanted to, he could have stood up there and colored in a coloring book. But I wanted to hear about fish. I wanted to close my eyes and see them swimming their silver sides along green rocks. I wanted to hear the river, feel it rush around my legs, flip the fly softly through the air, resting it on the tension of the river surface. Instead, I was up to my ears in foreign policy.

I wish I were the sort of person who liked everybody and everything. I feel so negative sometimes. I have friends who can listen to any song, watch any movie, or read any book, and they think everything is just great. I truly envy people who can do that. I say all of this because, as the author finally started reading from his new book, I didn't like it at all. I fought my critical nature but couldn't help but compare his new stuff to the genius of his previous work. His words were vaporous and cliché, trendy and full of sales pitches. They weren't his words, they were words that sell, words that tickle ears and reach a specified demographic.

In regard to spirituality, he surprised me by straying from his Christian convictions and bringing Muhammad into the light. He said that Muhammad was one of his heroes. I don't have so many problems with Muhammad, but I have problems with middle-aged white guys who grew up in America claiming Muhammad as a hero, not because Muhammad never did anything good (he did), but because calling Muhammad a hero is such an incredibly trendy thing to do. I know I am judging the guy's motives and all, but can you get any more trendy than subscribing to half-Christian, half-Islamic ideas? The guy was layering religious propositions like clothes in a J. Crew catalog.

The absolute most annoying thing about this guy's religious ideas was that they were so precisely where I was going with mine. It was like seeing my future pass before my eyes. I was on my way to becoming Captain Trendy Spiritual Writer. It was spooky.

Trendy Writer talked about how Khwaja Khandir is his fishing guide. He described Khwaja Khandir as the Islamic version of the Holy Spirit: Khwaja Khandir tells him where the fish are and teaches him things about life like how to manage his money or achieve inner peace or please his wife. It was all hokey and hoo-ha.

I felt as if I were being visited by the ghost of Christmas future, and the ghost was saying, "Hey, Don, you're going to end up like this guy: A yuppie Christian writer with no backbone!"

○   ○   ○

I think my desire to believe in a god other than Jesus had mostly to do with boredom. I wanted something new. I wanted something fresh to think about, to believe, to twiddle around in my mind. I understand the plight of the children of Israel, to be honest. Moses goes off to talk to God, he doesn't come back for a while, and so the people demand a god they can see and touch—a god they can worship with the absolute certainty it exists. So they build a golden cow (odd choice, but to each his own). Moses comes back from talking with God and finds the children of Israel worshiping a false god, so he goes postal. I imagined myself as the children of Israel when Moses comes down off of the mountain.

"What are you doing, Don?" Moses asks.

"Worshiping a golden cow."

"Why? Why would you reject the one true God?"

"Because I don't get to see Him or talk to Him. I am not even certain that He exists."

"Are you on crack, Don? Weren't you there when God parted the Red Sea? Weren't you there when God fed us from the ground, made water from a rock, led us with a cloud?" Moses screams.

"Calm down, Mosey. Listen, man, you always go up and talk to God and come back with a sunburn, and you have God hover around your tent in a cloud, and you have God turn your staff into a snake, and we get nothing. Nothing! It's not like we have this personal communication going with God, you know, Moses.

We are just sheep out here in the desert, and, honestly, we were better off as slaves to the Egyptians. That is where your God brought us. We need a god too. We need a god to worship. We need a god to touch and feel and interact with in a very personal way. So I made a cow. You can also wear it as a necklace."

"Don," Moses responds, "before I put you to death and send you home to the one true God, I want you to understand something. I want you to understand that God has never been nor ever will be invented. He is not a product of any sort of imagination. He does not obey trends. And God led us out of Egypt because you people cried out to Him. He was answering your prayers because He is a God of compassion. He could have left you to Satan. Don't complain about the way God answers your prayers. You are still living on an earth that is run by the devil. God has promised us a new land, and we will get there. Your problem is not that God is not fulfilling, your problem is that you are spoiled."

○ ○ ○

And Moses was right. God is not here to worship me, to mold Himself into something that will help me fulfill my level of comfort. I think part of my problem is that I want spirituality to be more close and more real. I understand why people wear crystals around their necks and why they perform chants and gaze at stars. They are lonely. I'm not talking about lonely for a lover or a friend. I mean lonely in the universal sense, lonely inside the understanding that we are tiny little people on a tiny little earth suspended in an endless void that echoes past stars and stars of stars. And it's not like God has a call-in radio show.

But as Trendy Writer read from his book that night at Powells, I thought about the Muslim babies dying in Afghanistan and

Pakistan. I thought about the economic crisis in Saudi Arabia and the children of Iraq who are being bombed because their ridiculous dictator won't cooperate with the United Nations. And then I thought about Khwaja Khandir, and I wondered what gave Trendy Writer the audacity to assume that Khwaja Khandir would have the time, or the desire, to take him fishing. Trendy Writer was trying to be hip and relevant, but in doing so he was cheapening the entire nation of Islam. And he was cheating on Jesus. He reminded me of Lot, who offered his daughters to the perverts because he wanted peace. Trendy Writer was sending out Muhammad and Jesus, asking them to hold hands so nobody would have to feel wrong or, rather, so he could have something fashionable to believe.

○　○　○

I talked to Tony about Trendy Writer. I told him how offensive it was that this guy was betraying Jesus and trampling all over Islam. When I told him the story of Trendy Writer, Tony closed his eyes and sighed. I asked him why he looked so troubled. He said it was because he felt convicted.

"Convicted about what, Tony?"

"I am convicted about what you are saying," he began. "Here is a guy using Islamic verbiage to make himself look spiritual, and yet he really hasn't researched or subscribed to the faith as it presents itself. He's just using it. Raping it for his own pleasure."

"Why are you convicted about that?" I asked him. "I've never heard you talk about Islamic ideas that way."

"I know," Tony said. "But I do the same thing with Jesus."

When Tony said that, it was as if truth came into the room and sat down with us. I felt as though Jesus were gently holding my head so He could work the plank out of my eye. Everything became clear. I realized in an instant that I desired false gods because Jesus wouldn't jump through my hoops, and I realized that, like Tony, my faith was about image and ego, not about practicing spirituality.

For me, Trendy Writer coming to town was the beginning of something. It was the beginning of my authentic Christianity. Trendy Writer, Khwaja Khandir, and Tony the Beat Poet were the seeds of change. I knew Christ, but I was not a practicing Christian. I had the image of a spiritual person, but I was bowing down to the golden cows of religiosity and philosophy. It was one of those enlightenments, one of those honest looks in the mirror in which there is no forgetting who you are. It was a moment without make-believe. After that moment, things started to get interesting.

Change

New Starts at Ancient Faith

THERE IS A TIME WHEN EVERY PERSON WHO encounters Jesus, who believes Jesus is the Son of God, decides that they will spend their life following Him. Some people, like the Apostle Paul, make this decision the minute they meet Him, the minute they become a Christian. Others, like the Apostle Peter, endure years of half-hearted commitment and spiritual confusion before leaping in with all their passion. Still others may enjoy some benefits of God's love and grace without entering into the true joy of a marriage with their maker.

Not long after I graduated from high school, I found myself leading a college group at a large church just outside Houston. I cherished the role, at first, because it was a place of honor. I studied the Bible for hours, putting talks together that students enjoyed. It started as a substitute teaching job. The college minister couldn't be there one week, so he asked me to fill in. When I was asked to speak again, I jumped at the chance like Homer Simpson at a donut. Pretty soon I was teaching all the time. I swam in the attention and the praise, I loved it, I lusted for it, I almost drowned in it.

The more attention I got, the stranger I became. I was on my way to having my own religious television show. Okay, that's a bit much, but you know what I mean. I was a smiler, a hand-shaker, a baby-kisser, a speech-giver. I said things like "God be with you," and "Lord bless you." I used clichés like a bad novelist.

I led the college group for a couple of years and enjoyed it at first, but it wasn't long before I felt like a phony. I got tired of myself. I didn't like to hear my own voice because I sounded like a talk-show host.

One afternoon I made an appointment with my pastor and told him I was leaving, that I was going into the world to get my thinking straight.

"How long will you be gone?" he asked.

"I don't know." I shrugged.

"Are you okay?"

"I think so. Maybe," I told him.

"Can you talk about it?" He looked concerned.

"No, not really."

"I understand you need a break. Why don't you take a couple weeks off."

"I was thinking longer," I told him.

"How long?"

"I don't know. Can you put a time limit on these things?"

"What things, Don?"

"I don't know," I told him, sort of staring out the window.

"Can you tell me how you feel?"

"No. I've tried to put words to it, you know, but I can't. I'm just really tired. Mentally drained. I feel like I am jumping through hoops or something. I don't feel like God is teaching through me. I feel like I am a fake person, you know. I say what I need to say, do what I need to do, but I don't really mean it."

"What does the real you want to say and do?" he asked me.

"I don't know. That is what the trip is about."

"Are you having a crisis of faith?" He looked concerned again.

"Maybe. What is a crisis of faith?" I asked him.

"Do you believe in God?"

"Yes. I want to go on a trip with Him."

"You aren't having any doubts at all?" he asked.

"No. I don't have any doubts about God or anything; it's just me. I feel like I am constantly saying things I don't mean. I tell people they should share their faith, but I don't feel like sharing my faith. I tell people they should be in the Word, but I am only in the Word because I have to teach the Word. I said to a guy the other day, 'God bless you.' What does that mean? I have been saying that stuff all my life, but what does that mean? Then I started thinking about all the crap I say. All the clichés, all the parroted slogans. I have become an infomercial for God, and I don't even use the product. I don't want to be who I am anymore."

"So you think you should go away," he clarified.

"Yes."

"Where will you go?"

"America."

"America?" He looked confused.

"America."

"We are in America right now, Don."

"Yeah, I know. But there are other parts to America. I'd like to see the other parts. I was looking at a map the other day, you know, and Texas was sort of brown with some green, a few hills, but then there were other places that were more green with big lumpy mountains. I'd like to go to those places."

"Do you think God is out there somewhere? Out there in the lumpy places?"

"I think God is everywhere."

"Then why do you have to leave?"

"Because I can't be here anymore. I don't feel whole here. I feel, well, partly whole. Incomplete. Tired. It has nothing to do with this church; it's all me. Something got crossed in the wires, and I became the person I should be and not the person I am. It feels like I should go back and get the person I am and bring him here to the person I should be. Are you following me at all? Do you know what I am talking about, about the green lumpy places?"

The conversation went on like this for about an hour. I went on and on about how the real me was out in the green lumpy places. I wasn't making any sense. I can't believe my pastor didn't call the guys with the white coats to take me away.

o   o   o

I suppose what I wanted back then is what every Christian wants, whether they understand themselves or not. What I wanted was God. I wanted tangible interaction. But even more than that, to be honest, I wanted to know who I was. I felt like a robot or an insect or a mysterious blob floating around in the universe. I believed if I could contact God, He would be able to explain who and why I was.

The days and weeks before a true commitment to Jesus can be terrible and lonely. I think I was feeling bitter about the human experience. I never asked to be human. Nobody came to the womb and explained the situation to me, asking for my permission to go into the world and live and breathe and eat and feel joy and pain. I started thinking about how odd it was to be human, how we are stuck inside this skin, forced to be attracted to the opposite sex, forced to eat food and use the rest room and then stuck to the earth by gravity. I think maybe I was going crazy or something. I spent an entire week feeling bitter because

I couldn't breathe underwater. I told God I wanted to be a fish. I also felt a little bitter about sleep. Why do we have to sleep? I wanted to be able to stay awake for as long as I wanted, but God had put me in this body that had to sleep. Life no longer seemed like an experience of freedom.

About twelve hours after I had the conversation with my pastor, a friend and I jumped into one of those Volkswagen camping vans and shoved off for the green lumpy places. A week into our American tour, we found ourselves at the bottom of the Grand Canyon, which is more lumpy than green, it turns out. It was a heck of a hike, let me tell you. I was in no shape to do it. So by the time I got to the bottom of that gargantuan hole in the ground, I was miserable. It was beautiful, don't get me wrong, but when your head is throbbing and you can't feel your lower half, you don't want to sit and reflect on how beautiful things are. Lumpy or not.

The canyon is more spectacular from the rim than from the river. Once in it, everything looks like Utah. As my friend and I fell asleep by the river, however, I had a cherished moment with God. I was in a lot of pain from the hike, so I was in no mood to mess around. There was no trying to impress Him, no speaking the right words. I simply began to pray and talk to God the way a child might talk to his father.

Beneath the billion stars and beside the river, I called out to God, softly.

"Hello?"

The stars were quiet. The river spoke in some other tongue, some vernacular for fish.

"I'm sorry, God. I'm sorry I got so confused about You, got so fake. I hope it's not too late anymore. I don't really know who I am, who You are, or what faith looks like. But if You want to talk, I'm here now. I could feel You convicting me when I was a kid, and I feel like You are trying to get through to me. But I feel like You are an alien or something, somebody far away."

Nothing from the stars. Fish language from the river. But as I lay there, talking to God, being real with Him, I began to feel a bit of serenity. It felt like I was apologizing to an old friend, someone with whom there had been a sort of bitterness, and the friend was saying it was okay, that he didn't think anything of it. It felt like I was starting over, or just getting started. That is the thing about giving yourself to God. Some people get really emotional about it, and some people don't feel much of anything except the peace they have after making an important decision. I felt a lot of peace.

There is something quite beautiful about the Grand Canyon at night. There is something beautiful about a billion stars held steady by a God who knows what He is doing. (They hang there, the stars, like notes on a page of music, free-form verse, silent mysteries swirling in the blue like jazz.) And as I lay there, it occurred to me that God is up there somewhere. Of course, I had always known He was, but this time I felt it, I realized it, the way a person realizes they are hungry or thirsty. The knowledge of God seeped out of my brain and into my heart. I imagined Him looking down on this earth, half angry because His beloved mankind had cheated on Him, had committed adultery, and yet hopelessly in love with her, drunk with love for her.

I know a little of why there is blood in my body, pumping life into my limbs and thought into my brain. I am wanted by God. He is wanting to preserve me, to guide me through the darkness of the shadow of death, up into the highlands of His presence and afterlife. I understand that I am temporary, in this shell of a thing on this dirt of an earth. I am being tempted by Satan, we are all being tempted by Satan, but I am preserved to tell those who do not know about our Savior and our Redeemer. This is why Paul had no questions. This is why he could be beaten one day, imprisoned the next, and released only to be beaten again and never ask God why. He understood the earth was fallen. He understood the rules of Rome could not save mankind, that mankind could not save itself; rather, it must be rescued, and he knew that he was not in the promised land, but still in the desert, and like Joshua and Caleb he was shouting, "Follow me and trust God!"

I see it now. I see that God was reaching out to Penny in the dorm room in France, and I see that the racism Laura and I talked about grows from the anarchy seed, the seed of the evil one. I could see Satan lashing out on the earth like a madman, setting tribes against each other in Rwanda, whispering in men's ears in the Congo so that they rape rather than defend their women. Satan is at work in the cults of the Third World, the economic chaos in Argentina, and the corporate-driven greed of American corporate executives.

I lay there under the stars and thought of what a great responsibility it is to be human. I am a human because God made me. I experience suffering and temptation because mankind chose to follow Satan. God is reaching out to me to rescue me. I am learning to trust Him, learning to live by His precepts that I might be preserved.

Belief

The Birth of Cool

MY MOST RECENT FAITH STRUGGLE IS NOT ONE of intellect. I don't really do that anymore. Sooner or later you just figure out there are some guys who don't believe in God and they can prove He doesn't exist, and some other guys who do believe in God and they can prove He does exist, and the argument stopped being about God a long time ago and now it's about who is smarter, and honestly I don't care. I don't believe I will ever walk away from God for intellectual reasons. Who knows anything anyway? If I walk away from Him, and please pray that I never do, I will walk away for social reasons, identity reasons, deep emotional reasons, the same reasons that any of us do anything.

My friend Julie Canlis from Seattle has this beautiful mother named Rachel who is small and petite and always remembers my name when I come for a visit. One morning I was sitting at the counter in the kitchen talking to Rachel about love and marriage, and she was gleaming about her husband a little, and I told her in one of those rare moments of vulnerability that I was scared to get married because I thought my wife might fall out of love with me, suddenly, after seeing a movie or reading a book or seeing me naked. You never know what might trigger these things. Rachael looked at me through the steam that was coming off her coffee and said, very wisely and comfortingly, that when a relationship is right, it is no more possible to wake up and want out of the marriage than it is to wake up and stop believing in God. What *is*, is what is, she said.

And that's when I realized that believing in God is as much like falling in love as it is like making a decision. Love is both something that happens to you *and* something you decide upon. And so I bring up that story about Julie's mom not because I want to talk about love, but because I want to talk some about belief. I have come to think that belief is something that happens to us too. Sure, there is some data involved, but mostly it is this deep, deep conviction, like what Julie's mom feels about her husband, this idea that life is about this thing, and it really isn't an option for it to be about something else.

I talked to a girl recently who said she liked Ethan Hawke, the actor and writer. He has a couple of novels out, and they are supposed to be really good, but I haven't read them. I know he is a fan of Douglas Coupland, which is a good thing if you ask me, so I'd probably like to read his stuff some day. But she was saying how much she liked him as a person, and I asked her why. She had to think quite a bit about it before she answered, but her answer was that he was an actor *and* a writer, not just an actor. He is an actor *and* a writer, and that is why you like him? I asked. Yes, she said. I thought that was profound. I was in a cranky mood so I asked her if she knew what he believed. What do you mean, she said. I mean do you know what he believes. I looked at her very squarely. Believes about what? she asked. Believes about anything, I said. Well, she told me as she sat back in her chair, I don't know. I don't know what he believes. Do you think he is cool? I asked her. Of course he is cool, she said.

And that is the thing that is so frustrating to me. I don't know if we really like pop-culture icons, follow them, buy into them because we resonate with what they believe or whether we buy into them because we think they are cool.

I was wondering the other day, why it is that we turn pop figures into idols? I have a theory, of course. I think we have this need to be cool, that there is this undercurrent in society that says some people are cool and some people aren't. And it is very, very important that we are cool. So, when we find somebody who is cool on television or on the radio, we associate ourselves with this person to feel valid ourselves. And the problem I have with this is that we rarely know what the person believes whom we are associating ourselves with. The problem with this is that it indicates there is less value in what people believe, what they stand for; it only matters that they are cool. In other words, who cares what I believe about life, I only care that I am cool. Because in the end, the undercurrent running through culture is not giving people value based upon what they believe and what they are doing to aid society, the undercurrent is deciding their value based upon whether or not they are cool.

I don't mean to pick on my friend who likes Ethan Hawke. She is very smart and has deep beliefs, but I just like the fact that I caught her being shallow. By shallow I mean she associated herself with somebody, thought somebody was "cool," and yet didn't know what he believed. I like that I caught her because she doesn't really live in that place, and I mostly do, and I hate that about myself and love that about her, so when she brought her head up to the surface, I wanted to point out the fact that she was in my neighborhood.

I had a crush on a girl who went to a rally in Chicago opposing

Bush's plan to attack Iraq. We were sitting around in my friend's living room and talking about it and she was in a huff and at one point raised her fist and said, "Down with Bush!" After that I didn't have a crush on her anymore. It wasn't because I like George W. Bush, it was because she had no idea why she didn't like George W. Bush. She only went to a rally and heard a good band and saw a lot of cool people with cool clothes and hippie haircuts. She decided what to believe based on whether other people who believed it were of a particular fashion that appealed to her. I saw myself in her quite a bit and that scared me. Girls like that make me want to marry Penny because Penny actually believes things. She lives them. I told Penny that I wanted to marry her, but she wasn't interested. I propose to Penny once a month now on the phone, but she just changes the subject.

The thing I have to work on in myself is this issue of belief. Gandhi believed Jesus when He said to turn the other cheek. Gandhi brought down the British Empire, deeply injured the caste system, and changed the world. Mother Teresa believed Jesus when He said everybody was priceless, even the ugly ones, the smelly ones, and Mother Teresa changed the world by show-ing them that a human being can be selfless. Peter finally believed the gospel after he got yelled at by Paul. Peter and Paul changed the world by starting small churches in godless towns.

Eminem believes he is a better rapper than other rappers. Profound. Let's all follow Eminem.

Here is the trick, and here is my point. Satan, who I believe exists as much as I believe Jesus exists, wants us to believe meaningless things for meaningless reasons. Can you imagine if Christians actu-ally believed that God was trying to rescue us from the pit of our own self-addiction? Can you imagine? Can you imagine what Americans would do if they understood over half the world was liv-ing in poverty? Do you think they would change the way they live, the products they purchase, and the politicians they elect? If we believed the right things, the true things, there wouldn't be very many problems on earth.

But the trouble with deep belief is that it costs something. And there is something inside me, some selfish beast of a subtle thing that doesn't like the truth at all because it carries responsibility, and if I actually believe these things I have to do something about them. It is so, so cumbersome to believe anything. And it isn't cool. I mean it's cool in a *Reality Bites, Welcome to Sarajevo,* Amnesty International sense, but that is only as good as dreadlocks. Chicks dig it to a point, but you can't be all about it; you also have to want a big house and expensive clothes because in the end, our beliefs are about as enduring as seasonal fashion. In the end, we like Ethan Hawke even though we don't know what he believes. Even our beliefs have become trend statements. We don't even believe things because we believe them anymore. We only believe things because they are cool things to believe.

The problem with Christian belief—I mean real Christian belief, the belief that there is a God and a devil and a heaven and a hell—is that it is not a fashionable thing to believe.

I had this idea once that if I could make Christianity cool, I could change the world, because if Christianity were cool then everybody would want to deal with their sin nature, and if everybody dealt with their sin nature then most of the world's problems would be solved. I decided that the best way to make Christianity cool was to use art. I attempted to write a short story about a fashionable Christian, so that everybody would want to be like him.

My fashionable Christian was deep. Deep water. A poet. He studied Thompson during his drug years, during the prostitute years. He had studied *The Hound of Heaven, In No Strange Land,* T. S. Eliot's *Four Quartets.* He smoked a pipe and read the

Romantics. And the Americans. Ginsberg's *"I watched the greatest minds of my generation descend into madness . . ."* was, to him, about sin nature. Part of him was about social justice. He could also skateboard and was in a rock band.

His name was Tom Toppins, and even though he had a goofy name, he overcame it because he rode an old Triumph motorcycle. In my story, Tom Toppins was casually dating a girl with blonde dreadlocks. She was a Buddhist; he was a Christian. He attended a Greek Orthodox church. She would go with him to church every once in a while, but he would not participate in her faith. He thought it was shallow, too much about fashion. He told her this over lunch at her loft apartment, and she exploded in anger. Then she cried, but he did not comfort her. He stood up and put on his jacket and lit up a cigarette and told her he was going to church. She screamed out, "How can you Christians maintain such an exclusive hold on truth!" He straightened his jacket while looking in a mirror and whispered to himself, *"'Cause that's the way it is, baby. That's the way it is."*

He walked out the door and left her weeping in agony, rubbing the belly of her little statue of Buddha. He didn't think of her again till the next day when he went by her apartment. Tom Toppins walked in and, though it was afternoon, found her sleeping, her face all red and wet with tears. He pulled a book of poems from his motorcycle jacket, Elizabeth Barrett Browning, and read to her from *Sonnets from the Portuguese* until she gently woke up. He lay down next to her and set her head on his free arm. She buried her head in his armpit and sobbed, but he didn't stop reading.

> My own beloved, who has lifted me
> From this drear flat of earth where I was thrown,
> And, in betwixt the languid ringlets, blown
> A life-breath, till the forehead hopefully

Shines out again, as all the angels see,
Before thy saving kiss! My own, my own,
Who camest to me when the world was gone,
And I who looked for only God, found *thee*.

I saw a movie the other day about all these people at this college back East, and it was a pretty grimy movie. There was a character in the movie, this guy who was a drug dealer and a jerk, and
everybody else in the movie loved him and wanted to have sex
with him. One of my housemates, Grant, was saying to me the
other day that girls always like bad guys. My friend Amy is like
that I think. And so was my friend Suzy, but Suzy said she got
over it and now she likes guys who are relatively nice and stable.

The thing about Tom Toppins, though, is that he really
believed things. He wasn't swayed. The same thing that was in
the drug dealer in that grimy movie that I absolutely do not rec-
ommend is the same thing that was in Tom Toppins: belief.
Drug Dealer Dude was not looking for somebody to pat him on
the back and teach him things, he was moving, going, sure of
something, even if it was all depravity, even if he was leading
people into hell. If you believe something, passionately, people
will follow you. People hardly care what you believe, as long as
you believe something. If you are passionate about something,
people will follow you because they think you know something
they don't, some clue to the meaning of the universe. Passion is
tricky, though, because it can point to nothing as easily as it
points to something. If a rapper is passionately rapping about
how great his rap is, his passion is pointing to nothing. He isn't
helping anything. His beliefs are self-serving and shallow. If a
rapper, however, is rapping about his community, about oppres-
sion and injustice, then he is passionate about a message, something outside himself. What people believe is important. What

people believe is more important than how they look, what their skills are, or their degree of passion. Passion about nothing is like pouring gasoline in a car without wheels. It isn't going to lead anybody anywhere.

My friend Andrew the Protester believes things. Andrew goes to protests where he gets pepper-sprayed, and he does it because he believes in being a voice of change. My Republican friends get frustrated when I paint Andrew as a hero, but I like Andrew because he actually believes things that cost him something. Even if I disagree with Andrew, I love that he is willing to sacrifice for what he believes. And I love that his beliefs are about social causes.

Andrew says it is not enough to be politically active. He says legislation will never save the world. On Saturday mornings Andrew feeds the homeless. He sets up a makeshift kitchen on a sidewalk and makes breakfast for people who live on the street. He serves coffee and sits with his homeless friends and talks and laughs, and if they want to pray he will pray with them. He's a flaming liberal, really. The thing about it is, though, Andrew believes this is what Jesus wants him to do. Andrew does not believe in empty passion.

All great Christian leaders are simple thinkers. Andrew doesn't cloak his altruism within a trickle-down economic theory that allows him to spend fifty dollars on a round of golf to feed the economy and provide jobs for the poor. He actually believes that when Jesus says feed the poor, He means you should do this directly.

Andrew is the one who taught me that what I believe is not what I say I believe; what I believe is what I do.

I used to say that I believed it was important to tell people about Jesus, but I never did. Andrew very kindly explained that if I do not introduce people to Jesus, then I don't believe Jesus is an important person. It doesn't matter what I say. Andrew said

I should not live like a politician, but like a Christian. Like I said, Andrew is a simple thinker.

o   o   o

A friend of mine, a young pastor who recently started a church, talks to me from time to time about the new face of church in America—about the postmodern church. He says the new church will be different from the old one, that we will be relevant to culture and the human struggle. I don't think any church has ever been relevant to culture, to the human struggle, unless it believed in Jesus and the power of His gospel. If the supposed new church believes in trendy music and cool Web pages, then it is not relevant to culture either. It is just another tool of Satan to get people to be passionate about nothing.

o   o   o

Tony asked me one time if there was anything I would die for. I had to think about it for a long time, and even after thinking about it for a couple of days I had a short list. In the end there weren't very many principles I would die for. I would die for the gospel because I think it is the only revolutionary idea known to man. I would die for Penny, for Laura and Tony. I would die for Rick. Andrew would say that dying for something is easy because it is associated with glory. Living for something, Andrew would say, is the hard thing. Living for something extends beyond fashion, glory, or recognition. We live for what we believe, Andrew would say.

If Andrew the Protester is right, if I live what I believe, then I don't believe very many noble things. My life testifies that the first thing I believe is that I am the most important person in the world. My life testifies to this because I care more about my food and shelter and happiness than about anybody else.

I am learning to believe better things. I am learning to believe that other people exist, that fashion is not truth; rather, Jesus is the most important figure in history, and the gospel is the most powerful force in the universe. I am learning not to be passionate about empty things, but to cultivate passion for justice, grace, truth, and communicate the idea that Jesus likes people and even loves them.

11

Confession

Coming Out of the Closet

WHEN I WAS IN SUNDAY SCHOOL AS A KID, MY
teacher put a big poster on the wall that was shaped in a circle like
a target. She had us write names of people we knew who weren't
Christians on little pieces of paper, and she pinned the names to
the outer circle of the target. She said our goal, by the end of the
year, was to move those names from the outer ring of the circle,
which represented their distance from knowing Jesus, to the inner
ring, which represented them having come into a relationship
with Jesus. I thought the strategy was beautiful because it gave us
a goal, a visual.

I didn't know any people who weren't Christians, but I was a
child with a fertile imagination so I made up some names; Thad
Thatcher was one and William Wonka was another. My teacher
didn't believe me which I took as an insult, but nonetheless, the
class was excited the very next week when both Thad and William
had become Christians in a dramatic conversion experience that
included the dismantling of a large satanic cult and underground
drug ring. There was also levitation involved.

Even though they didn't exist, Thad and William were the only people to become Christians all year. Nobody else I knew became a Christian for a very long time, mostly because I didn't tell anybody about Jesus except when I was drunk at a party, and that was only because so many of my reservations were down, and even then nobody understood me because I was either crying or slurring my words.

o   o   o

When I moved downtown to attend Imago-Dei, the church Rick started, he was pretty serious about loving people regardless of whether they considered Jesus the Son of God or not, and Rick wanted to love them because they were either hungry, thirsty, or lonely. The human struggle bothered Rick, as if something was broken in the world and we were supposed to hold our palms against the wound. He didn't really see evangelism, or whatever you want to call it, as a target on a wall in which the goal is to get people to agree with us about the meaning of life. He saw evangelism as reaching a felt need. I thought this was beautiful and frightening. I thought it was beautiful because I had this same need; I mean, I really knew I needed Jesus like I need water or food, and yet it was frightening because Christianity is so stupid to so much of our culture, and I absolutely hate bothering people about this stuff.

So much of me believes strongly in letting everybody live their own lives, and when I share my faith, I feel like a network marketing guy trying to build my down line.

Some of my friends who aren't Christians think that Christians are insistent and demanding and intruding, but that isn't the case. Those folks are the squeaky wheel. Most Christians have enormous respect for the space and freedom of others; it is only that they have found a joy in Jesus they want to share. There is the tension.

In a recent radio interview I was sternly asked by the host, who did not consider himself a Christian, to defend Christianity. I told him that I couldn't do it, and moreover, that I didn't want to defend the term. He asked me if I was a Christian, and I told him yes. "Then why don't you want to defend Christianity?" he asked, confused. I told him I no longer knew what the term meant. Of the hundreds of thousands of people listening to his show that day, some of them had terrible experiences with Christianity; they may have been yelled at by a teacher in a Christian school, abused by a minister, or browbeaten by a Christian parent. To them, the term *Christianity* meant something that no Christian I know would defend. By fortifying the term, I am only making them more and more angry. I won't do it. Stop ten people on the street and ask them what they think of when they hear the word *Christianity,* and they will give you ten different answers. How can I defend a term that means ten different things to ten different people? I told the radio show host that I would rather talk about Jesus and how I came to believe that Jesus exists and that he likes me. The host looked back at me with tears in his eyes. When we were done, he asked me if we could go get lunch together. He told me how much he didn't like Christianity but how he had always wanted to believe Jesus was the Son of God.

○   ○   ○

For me, the beginning of sharing my faith with people began by throwing out Christianity and embracing Christian spirituality, a nonpolitical mysterious system that can be experienced but not explained. *Christianity,* unlike *Christian spirituality,* was not a term that excited me. And I could not in good conscious tell a friend about a faith that didn't excite me. I couldn't share something I wasn't experiencing. And I wasn't experiencing Christianity. It didn't do anything for me at all. It felt like math, like a system of rights and wrongs and political beliefs, but it wasn't mysterious; it wasn't God reaching out of heaven to do wonderful things in my life. And if I would have shared Christianity with somebody, it would have felt mostly like I was trying to get somebody to agree with me rather than meet God. I could no longer share anything about Christianity, but I loved talking about Jesus and the spirituality that goes along with a relationship with Him.

Tony the Beat Poet says the church is like a wounded animal these days. He says we used to have power and influence, but now we don't, and so many of our leaders are upset about this and acting like spoiled children, mad because they can't have their way. They disguise their actions to look as though they are standing on principle, but it isn't that, Tony says, it's bitterness. They want to take their ball and go home because they have to sit the bench. Tony and I agreed that what God wants us to do is sit the bench in humility and turn the other cheek like Gandhi, like Jesus. We decided that the correct place to share our faith was from a place of humility and love, not from a desire for power.

o   o   o

Each year at Reed they have a festival called Ren Fayre. They shut down the campus so students can party. Security keeps the authorities away, and everybody gets pretty drunk and high, and some people get naked. Friday night is mostly about getting drunk, and Saturday night is about getting high. The school brings in White Bird, a medical unit that specializes in treating bad drug trips. The students create special lounges with black lights and television screens to enhance kids' mushroom trips.

Some of the Christian students in our little group decided this was a pretty good place to come out of the closet, letting everybody know there were a few Christians on campus. Tony the Beat Poet and I were sitting around in my room one afternoon talking about what to do, how to explain who we were to a group of students who, in the past, had expressed hostility toward Christians. Like our friends, we felt like Ren Fayre was the time to do this. I said we should build a confession booth in the middle of campus and paint a sign on it that said "Confess your sins." I said this because I knew a lot of people would be sinning, and Christian spirituality begins by confessing our sins and repenting. I also said it as a joke. But Tony thought it was brilliant. He sat there on my couch with his mind in the clouds, and he was scaring the crap out of me because, for a second, then for a minute, I actually believed he wanted to do it.

"Tony," I said very gently.

"What?" he said, with a blank stare at the opposite wall.

"We are not going to do this," I told him. He moved his gaze down the wall and directly into my eyes. A smile came across his face.

"Oh, we are, Don. We certainly are. We are going to build a confession booth!"

We met in Commons—Penny, Nadine, Mitch, Iven, Tony, and I. Tony said I had an idea. They looked at me. I told them that Tony was lying and I didn't have an idea at all. They looked at Tony. Tony gave me a dirty look and told me to tell them the idea. I told them I had a stupid idea that we couldn't do without getting attacked. They leaned in. I told them that we should build a confession booth in the middle of campus and paint a sign on it that said "Confess your sins." Penny put her hands over her mouth. Nadine smiled. Iven laughed. Mitch started drawing the designs for the booth on a napkin. Tony nodded his head. I wet my pants.

"They may very well burn it down," Nadine said.

"I will build a trapdoor," Mitch said with his finger in the air.

"I like it, Don." Iven patted me on the back.

"I don't want anything to do with it," Penny said.

"Neither do I," I told her.

"Okay, you guys." Tony gathered everybody's attention. "Here's the catch." He leaned in a little and collected his thoughts. "We are not actually going to accept confessions." We all looked at him in confusion. He continued, "We are going to confess to them. We are going to confess that, as followers of Jesus, we have not been very loving; we have been bitter, and for that we are sorry. We will apologize for the Crusades, we will apologize for televangelists, we will apologize for neglecting the poor and the lonely, we will ask them to forgive us, and we will tell them that in our selfishness, we have misrepresented Jesus on this campus. We will tell people who come into the booth that Jesus loves them."

All of us sat there in silence because it was obvious that something beautiful and true had hit the table with a thud. We all thought it was a great idea, and we could see it in each other's eyes. It would feel so good to apologize, to apologize for the Crusades, for Columbus and the genocide he committed in the Bahamas in the name of God, apologize for the missionaries who landed in Mexico and came up through the West slaughtering Indians in the name of Christ. I wanted so desperately to say that none of this was Jesus, and I wanted so desperately to apologize for the many ways I had misrepresented the Lord. I could feel that I had betrayed the Lord by judging, by not being willing to love the people He had loved and only giving lip service to issues of human rights.

For so much of my life I had been defending Christianity because I thought to admit that we had done any wrong was to discredit the religious system as a whole, but it isn't a religious system, it is people following Christ; and the important thing to do, the right thing to do, was to apologize for getting in the way of Jesus.

Later I had a conversation with a very arrogant Reed professor in the parking lot in which he asked me what brought me to Reed. I told him I was auditing a class but was really there to interact with the few Christians who studied at Reed. The professor asked me if I was a Christian evangelist. I told him I didn't think I was, that I wouldn't consider myself an evangelist. He went on to compare my work to that of Captain Cook, who had attempted to bring Western values to indigenous people of Hawaii. He looked me in the eye and said the tribes had killed Cook.

He did not wish me a greater fate at Reed.

All the way home on my motorcycle I fumed and imagined beating the professor into a pulp right there in the parking lot. I could see his sly smile, his intellectual pride. Sure, Christians had done terrible things to humanity, but I hadn't. I had never killed anybody at all. And those people weren't following Jesus when they committed those crimes against humanity. They were government people, and government always uses God to manipulate the masses into following them.

Both Clinton and Bush claim to be followers of Jesus. Anybody who wants to get their way says that Jesus supports their view. But that isn't Jesus' fault. Tony had come to campus a few days earlier, a bit sad in the face. He had seen a bumper sticker on one of the cars in the parking lot that read "Too bad we can't feed Christians to the lions anymore."

I prayed about getting in the confession booth. I wondered whether I could apologize and mean it. I wondered whether I could humble myself to a culture that, to some degree, had wronged us. But I could see in Penny's face, in Iven's eyes, that this was what they wanted; they wanted to love these people, their friends, and it didn't matter to them what it cost. They didn't care how much they had been hurt, and they certainly had more scars than either Tony or I, and so we bought the wood and stored it in my garage, and Friday night we went to the Thesis parade and watched everybody get drunk and beat drums and dance in the spray of beer. Tony and I dressed like monks and smoked pipes and walked among the anarchy, becoming soaked in all the alcohol spewing from within the crowds. People would come up to us and ask what we were doing, and we told them that the next day we would be on campus to take confessions. They looked at us in amazement, sometimes asking us whether we were serious. We told them to come and see us, that we were going to build a confession booth.

The next morning, while everybody was sleeping off their hangovers, Mitch, Tony, and I started building the thing. Mitch had the plans drawn out. The booth was huge, much bigger than I expected, almost like a shed complete with a slanted roof and two small sections inside, one for the monk and the other for the confessor. We built a half-high wall between the two rooms and installed a curtain so the confessor could easily get in and out. On our side we installed a door with a latch so nobody could come in and drag us away. Nadine painted "Confession Booth" in large letters on the outside of the booth.

As the campus started to gather energy, people walking along the sidewalk would ask what we were doing. They stood there looking at the booth in wonder. "What are we supposed to do?" they would ask. "Confess your sins," we told them. "To who?" they would say. "To God," we would tell them. "There is no God," they would explain. Some of them told us this was the boldest thing they had ever seen. All of them were kind, which surprised us.

I stood there outside the booth as a large blue mob started running across campus, all of them, more than a hundred people, naked and painted with blue paint. They ran by the booth screaming and waving. I waved back. Naked people look funny when they are for-real naked, outside-a-magazine naked.

Saturday evening at Ren Fayre is alive and fun. The sun goes down over campus, and shortly after dark they shoot fireworks over the tennis courts. Students lay themselves out on a hill and laugh and point in bleary-eyed fascination. The highlight of the evening is a glow opera that packs the amphitheater with students and friends. The opera is designed to enhance mushroom trips. The actors wear all black and carry colorful puppets and cutouts that come alive in the black light. Everybody ooohs and aaahs.

The party goes till nearly dawn, so though it was late we started working the booth. We lit tiki torches and mounted them in the ground just outside the booth. Tony and Iven were saying that I should go first, which I didn't want to do, but I played bold and got in the booth. I sat on a bucket and watched the ceiling and the smoke from my pipe gather in the dark corners like ghosts. I could hear the rave happening in the student center across campus. I was picturing all the cool dancers, the girls in white shirts moving through the black light, the guys with the turntables in the loft, the big screen with the swirling images and all that energy coming out of the speakers, pounding through everybody's bodies, getting everybody up and down, up and down. *Nobody is going to confess anything,* I thought. *Who wants to stop dancing to confess their sins?* And I realized that this was a bad idea, that none of this was God's idea. Nobody was going to get angry, but nobody was going to care very much either.

There is nothing relevant about Christian spirituality, I kept thinking. God, if He is even there, has no voice in this place. Everybody wants to have a conversation about truth, but there isn't any truth anymore. The only truth is what is cool, what is on television, what protest is going on on what block, and it doesn't matter the issue; it only matters who is going to be there and will there be a party later and can any of us feel like we are relevant while we are at the party. And in the middle of it we are like Mormons on bikes. I sat there wondering whether any of this was true, whether Christian spirituality was even true at all. You never question the truth of something until you have to explain it to a skeptic. I didn't feel like explaining it very much. I didn't feel like being in the booth or wearing that stupid monk outfit. I wanted to go to the rave. Everybody in there was cool, and we were just religious.

I was going to tell Tony that I didn't want to do it when he opened the curtain and said we had our first customer.

"What's up, man?" Duder sat himself on the chair with a smile on his face. He told me my pipe smelled good.

"Thanks," I said. I asked him his name, and he said his name was Jake. I shook his hand because I didn't know what to do, really.

"So, what is this? I'm supposed to tell you all of the juicy gossip I did at Ren Fayre, right?" Jake said.

"No."

"Okay, then what? What's the game?" He asked.

"Not really a game. More of a confession thing."

"You want me to confess my sins, right?"

"No, that's not what we're doing, really."

"What's the deal, man? What's with the monk outfit?"

"Well, we are, well, a group of Christians here on campus, you know."

"I see. Strange place for Christians, but I am listening."

"Thanks," I told him. He was being very patient and gracious. "Anyway, there is this group of us, just a few of us who were thinking about the way Christians have sort of wronged people over time. You know, the Crusades, all that stuff . . ."

"Well, I doubt you personally were involved in any of that, man."

"No, I wasn't," I told him. "But the thing is, we are followers of Jesus. We believe that He is God and all, and He represented

certain ideas that we have sort of not done a good job at representing. He has asked us to represent Him well, but it can be
very hard."

"I see," Jake said.

"So there is this group of us on campus who wanted to confess to you."

"You are confessing to me!" Jake said with a laugh.

"Yeah. We are confessing to you. I mean, I am confessing to
you."

"You're serious." His laugh turned to something of a straight
face.

I told him I was. He looked at me and told me I didn't have
to. I told him I did, and I felt very strongly in that moment that
I was supposed to tell Jake that I was sorry about everything.

"What are you confessing?" he asked.

I shook my head and looked at the ground. "Everything," I
told him.

"Explain," he said.

"There's a lot. I will keep it short," I started. "Jesus said to feed
the poor and to heal the sick. I have never done very much about
that. Jesus said to love those who persecute me. I tend to lash out,
especially if I feel threatened, you know, if my ego gets threatened.
Jesus did not mix His spirituality with politics. I grew up doing that.
It got in the way of the central message of Christ. I know that was
wrong, and I know that a lot of people will not listen to the words
of Christ because people like me, who know Him, carry our own
agendas into the conversation rather than just relaying the message
Christ wanted to get across. There's a lot more, you know."

"It's all right, man," Jake said, very tenderly. His eyes were
starting to water.

"Well," I said, clearing my throat, "I am sorry for all of that."

"I forgive you," Jake said. And he meant it.

"Thanks," I told him.

He sat there and looked at the floor, then into the fire of a candle. "It's really cool what you guys are doing," he said. "A lot of people need to hear this."

"Have we hurt a lot of people?" I asked him.

"You haven't hurt me. I just think it isn't very popular to be a Christian, you know. Especially at a place like this. I don't think too many people have been hurt. Most people just have a strong reaction to what they see on television. All these well-dressed preachers supporting the Republicans."

"That's not the whole picture," I said. "That's just television. I have friends who are giving their lives to feed the poor and defend the defenseless. They are doing it for Christ."

"You really believe in Jesus, don't you?" he asked me.

"Yes, I think I do. Most often I do. I have doubts at times, but mostly I believe in Him. It's like there is something in me that causes me to believe, and I can't explain it."

"You said earlier that there was a central message of Christ. I don't really want to become a Christian, you know, but what is that message?"

"The message is that man sinned against God and God gave the world over to man, and that if somebody wanted to be rescued out of that, if somebody for instance finds it all very empty, that Christ will rescue them if they want; that if they ask forgiveness for being a part of that rebellion then God will forgive them."

"What is the deal with the cross?" Jake asked.

"God says the wages of sin is death," I told him. "And Jesus died so that none of us would have to. If we have faith in that then we are Christians."

"That is why people wear crosses?" he asked.

"I guess. I think it is sort of fashionable. Some people believe that if they have a cross around their neck or tatooed on them or something, it has some sort of mystical power."

"Do you believe that?" Jake asked.

"No," I answered. I told him that I thought mystical power came through faith in Jesus.

"What do you believe about God?" I asked him.

"I don't know. I guess I didn't believe for a long time, you know. The science of it is so sketchy. I guess I believe in God though. I believe somebody is responsible for all of this, this world we live in. It is all very confusing."

"Jake, if you want to know God, you can. I am just saying if you ever want to call on Jesus, He will be there."

"Thanks, man. I believe that you mean that." His eyes were watering again. "This is cool what you guys are doing," he repeated. "I am going to tell my friends about this."

"I don't know whether to thank you for that or not," I laughed. "I have to sit here and confess all my crap."

He looked at me very seriously. "It's worth it," he said. He shook my hand, and when he left the booth there was somebody else ready to get in. It went like that for a couple of hours. I talked to about thirty people, and Tony took confessions on a picnic table outside the booth. Many people wanted to hug when we were done. All of the people who visited the booth were grateful and gracious. I was being changed through the process. I went in with doubts and came out believing so strongly in Jesus I was ready to die and be with Him. I think that night was the beginning of change for a lot of us.

Iven started taking a group to a local homeless shelter to feed the poor, and he often had to turn students away because the van wouldn't hold more than twenty or so. We held an event called Poverty Day where we asked students to live on less than three dollars a day to practice solidarity with the poor. More than one hundred students participated. Penny spoke in Vollum Lounge on the topic of poverty in India, and more than seventy-five students came. Before any of this, our biggest even had about ten people. We hosted an evening where we asked students to come and voice their hostility against Christians. We answered questions about what we believed and explained our love for people, for the hurting, and we apologized again for our own wrongs against humanity and asked for forgiveness from the Reed community. We enjoyed the new friendships we received, and at one time had four different Bible studies on campus specifically for people who did not consider themselves Christians. We watched a lot of students take a second look at Christ. But mostly, we as Christians felt right with the people around us. Mostly we felt forgiven and grateful.

Sometime around two or three in the morning, the night we took confessions, I was walking off the campus with my monk robe under my arm, and when I got to the large oak trees on the outskirts of the font lawn, I turned and looked at the campus. It all looked so smart and old, and I could see the lights coming out of the Student Center, and I could hear the music thumping. There were kids making out on the lawn and chasing each other down the sidewalks. There was laughing and dancing and throwing up.

I felt very strongly that Jesus was relevant in this place. I felt very strongly that if He was not relevant here then He was not relevant anywhere. I felt very peaceful in that place and very sober. I felt very connected to God because I had confessed so much to so many people and had gotten so much off my chest and I had been forgiven by the people I had wronged with my indifference and judgmentalism. I was going to sit there for a little while, but it was cold and the grass was damp. I went home and fell asleep on the couch and the next morning made coffee and sat on the porch at Graceland and wondered whether the things that happened the night before had actually happened. I was out of the closet now. A Christian. So many years before I had made amends to God, but now I had made amends to the world. I was somebody who was willing to share my faith. It felt kind of cool, kind of different. It was very relieving.

12

Church

How I Go Without Getting Angry

IT SHOULD BE SAID I AM AN INDEPENDENT PERSON. I don't like institutionalized anything. I don't like corporations. I am not saying institutions and corporations are wrong, or bad; I am only saying I don't like them. Some people don't like classical music, some people don't like pizza, I don't like institutions. My dislike might stem from a number of things, from the nonpersonal feel I get when I walk into a corporate office or the voice-mail system I encounter when I call my bank. It might be the nonengaged look on every fast-food worker's face or the phone calls I receive in the middle of dinner asking me what long-distance carrier I use. Those people never want to just talk; they always have an agenda.

My dislike for institutions is mostly a feeling, though, not something that can be explained. There are upsides to institutions, of course. Tradition, for example. The corridors at Harvard, rich with history, thick with thought, the availability of good, hot Starbucks coffee at roughly thirty locations within five miles of my home. And what about all those jobs? Without the corporate machine, where would people work? I suppose we need them. The institutions. The corporations. But mostly I don't like them. I don't have to like them either. It's my right.

I don't like church, either, for the same reason. Or I should say I didn't like church. I like attending a Catholic service every once in a while, but I think that is because it feels different to me. I grew up Baptist. I like watching religious television every once in a while. It's better than Comedy Central. I want to study psychology so I can sit in front of religious television and figure out these people's problems. For a while I was very fascinated with televangelists. I couldn't afford a television ministry but I had a computer, so I would go into Christian chat rooms and try to heal people. It was funny at first, but it got boring.

Some of my friends have left their churches and gone Greek Orthodox. I think that sounds cool. Greek Orthodox. Unless you are Greek. Then it sounds like that is where you are supposed to go, as though you are a conformist. If I were Greek, I would never go to a Greek Orthodox church. If I were Greek, I would go to a Baptist church. Everybody there would think I was exotic and cool.

o   o   o

I go to a church now that I love. I never thought I would say that about a church. I never thought I could love a church. But I love this one. It is called Imago-Dei, which means "Image of God" in Latin. Latin is exotic and cool.

In the churches I used to go to, I felt like I didn't fit in. I always felt like the adopted kid, as if there was "room at the table for me." Do you know what I mean? I was accepted but not understood. There was room at the table for me, but I wasn't in the family.

It doesn't do any good to bash churches, so I am not making

blanket statements against the church as a whole. I have only been involved in a few churches, but I had the same tension with each of them; that's the only reason I bring it up.

○   ○   ○

Here are the things I didn't like about the churches I went to. First: I felt like people were trying to sell me Jesus. I was a salesman for a while, and we were taught that you are supposed to point out all the benefits of a product when you are selling it. That is how I felt about some of the preachers I heard speak. They were always pointing out the benefits of Christian faith. That rubbed me wrong. It's not that there aren't benefits, there are, but did they have to talk about spirituality like it's a vacuum cleaner. I never felt like Jesus was a product. I wanted Him to be a person. Not only that, but they were always pointing out how great the specific church was. The bulletin read like a brochure for Amway. They were always saying how life-changing some conference was going to be. Life-changing? What does that mean? It sounded very suspicious. I wish they would just tell it to me straight rather than trying to sell me on everything. I felt like I got bombarded with commercials all week and then went to church and got even more.

And yet another thing about the churches I went to: They seemed to be parrots for the Republican Party. Do we have to tow the party line on every single issue? Are the Republicans that perfect? I just felt like, in order to be a part of the family, I had to think George W. Bush was Jesus. And I didn't. I didn't think that Jesus really agreed with a lot of the policies of the Republican Party or for that matter the Democratic Party. I felt like Jesus was a religious figure, not a political figure. I heard my pastor say once, when there were only a few of us standing around, that he hated Bill Clinton. I can understand not liking Clinton's policies, but I want my spirituality to rid me of hate, not give me reason for it. I couldn't deal with that. That is one of the main reasons I walked away. I felt like, by going to this particular church, I was a pawn for the Republicans. Meanwhile, the Republicans did not give a crap about the causes of Christ.

Only one more thing that bugged me, then I will shut up about it. War metaphor. The churches I attended would embrace war metaphor. They would talk about how we are in a battle, and I agreed with them, only they wouldn't clarify that we were battling poverty and hate and injustice and pride and the powers of darkness. They left us thinking that our war was against liberals and homosexuals. Their teaching would have me believe I was the good person in the world and the liberals were the bad people in the world. Jesus taught that we are all bad and He is good, and He wants to rescue us because there is a war going on and we are hostages in that war. The truth is we are supposed to love the hippies, the liberals, and even the Democrats, and that God wants us to think of them as more important than ourselves. Anything short of this is not true to the teachings of Jesus.

o o o

So I was speaking at this twenty-something ministry, speaking to about fifty or so people on Sunday nights at a church in the suburbs, all the while dying inside. I wasn't even attending the main worship service anymore. The pastor who was in charge of the college group asked me why I wasn't coming to church. He was very kind and sympathetic and said he missed seeing me there.

Tony the Beat Poet says I am not good with diplomacy. He says I speak my mind too much and I should consider the ramifications of my words. I can be a real jerk without even realizing it. I told the guy it was hard for me to go to church without getting angry, and I think he took that personally. I tried to explain how I felt, but I was speaking a different language. I felt stupid, too, like some bitter idiot all wet and wanting everybody to cater to me, to my ideas about who Jesus is and was and the way He wants us to live.

About that time I started asking God to help me find a church where I would fit.

I had this friend from Seattle named Mark who was the pastor of a pretty cool church near the University of Washington, in the village. He had a lot of artists going to his church and a lot of hippies and yuppies and people who listen to public radio. I went up and visited him one time, and I loved the community he had put together. I felt like I could breathe for the first time in years. Visiting Mark's church in Seattle helped me realize I wasn't alone in the world. I would talk to my friends about his church, to my friends at the church I was attending, but they didn't get it.

Mark had written several articles for secular magazines and had been interviewed a few times on the radio and had gotten this reputation as a pastor who said cusswords. It is true that Mark said a lot of cusswords. I don't know why he did it. He didn't become a Christian till he was in college, so maybe he didn't know he wasn't supposed to say cusswords and be a pastor. I think some of my friends believed that it was the goal of the devil to get people to say cusswords, so they thought Mark was possessed or something, and they told me I should not really get into anything he was a part of. Because of the cusswords. But like I said, I was dying inside, and even though Mark said cusswords, he was telling a lot of people about Jesus, and he was being socially active, and he seemed to love a lot of people the church was neglecting, like liberals and fruit nuts. About the time I was praying that God would help me find a church, I got a call from Mark the Cussing Pastor, and he said he had a close friend who was moving to Portland to start a church and that I should join him.

Rick and I got together over coffee, and I thought he was hilarious. He was big, a football player out of Chico State. At the time we both chewed tobacco, so we had that in common. He could do a great Tony Soprano voice, sort of a Mafia thing. He would do this routine where he pretended to be a Mafia boss who was planting a church. He said a few cusswords but not as bad as Mark. Rick said there were a few people meeting at his house to talk about what it might look like to start a church in Portland, and he invited me to come. I could feel that God was answering my prayer so I went. There were only about eight of us, mostly kids, mostly teens just out of high school. I felt like I was at a youth group, honestly. I didn't think the thing was going to fly. Rick's wife made us coffee, and we sat around his living room, and Rick read us some statistics about how very many churches have moved out of the cities and into the suburbs and said how he wanted us to plant in the city. Rick really wanted to redeem the image of the church to people who had false conceptions about it.

Pretty soon there were twenty or so of us, so we got this little chapel at a college near downtown and started having church. It felt funny at church, you know, because there were only twenty of us and it was mostly just kids, but I still believed this was how God was going to answer my prayer.

We didn't grow much, to be honest. We stayed at about thirty or so, all Christians who had moved to Imago from other churches. I know that numbers shouldn't matter very much, but to be honest I kind of wanted Imago to grow because I wanted my friends at my old church to know we were successful; but we didn't grow, we stayed at about thirty.

We'd meet on Sunday nights and then again on Wednesday nights for prayer. A lot less people showed up for prayer. There were only about ten of us, and it was pretty boring. It felt like an AA meeting gone bad. We'd sit around and talk about the crap in our lives, and then we'd pray for a little while, and then we would go home. One night Rick showed up sort of beaten-looking. He had been to some sort of pastors reception where a guy spoke about how the church has lost touch with people who didn't know about Jesus. Rick said he was really convicted about this and asked us if we thought we needed to repent and start loving people who were very different from us. We all told him yes, we did, but I don't think any of us knew what that meant. Rick said he thought it meant we should live missional lives, that we should intentionally befriend people who are different from us. I didn't like the sound of that, to be honest. I didn't want to befriend somebody just to trick them into going to my church. Rick said that was not what he was talking about. He said he was talking about loving people just because they exist—homeless people and Gothic people and gays and fruit nuts. And then I liked the sound of it. I liked the idea of loving people just to love them, not to get them to come to church. If the subject of church came up, I could tell them about Imago, but until then, who cared. So we started praying every week that God would teach us to live missional lives, to notice people who needed to be loved.

Lots of people started coming to church after that. I don't know why, honestly, except that we all agreed we would love people and be nice to them and listen and make friends. As we grew, we had to move into another building and then another one after that and then to another one until we started renting this big, super-old, beautiful church with stained glass windows and a domed ceiling. Shortly after we moved in there we had to go to two services. All of this happened in a couple of years, and now Imago has about five hundred people coming and lots of them look like rock stars, but they are all brilliant and spiritual. I love the community so much it's hard to describe. I have never felt such a feeling of family in all my life. I felt like I had nothing in terms of community and God brought a community up out of the ground, out of pure nothing like a magic trick.

Like I said before, I never thought I would love church. But here is what I love about Imago-Dei.

First: It is spiritual. What I mean is the people at Imago pray and fast about things. It took me a while to understand that the answer to problems was not marketing or program but rather spirituality. If we needed to reach youth, we wouldn't do a pizza feed and a game night, we would get together and pray and fast and ask God what to do. God led some guys to start a homeless teen outreach downtown, and now they feed about one hundred homeless teenagers every week. It is the nuttiest youth group you will ever see, but that is what God said to do. I love that sort of thing because rather than the church serving itself, the church is serving the lost and lonely. It gives me chills when I think about it because it is that beautiful of a thing.

Second: Art. Imago supports the arts. Rick isn't much of an artist, but he turned things over to a guy named Peter Jenkins, who created the drawings for this book. Peter started an "artistery" where artists live and create art, teach art, and encourage people to be creative. Peter recently held a gallery opening in a local coffeehouse, and all the art was created by people who attend Imago. Artists feel at home at Imago. I even led a short-story group where we wrote short stories and then had a reading under Christmas lights and candles over at the artistery. I think there are artists at a lot of churches who don't have an outlet, and by creating an outlet, the church gives artists a chance to express themselves and in return the church gets free stuff to put on their walls. Creating an arts group at a church is a great idea.

Third: Community. Rick is very, very serious about people living together, eating together, and playing together. He encourages young single people to get houses and live with each other. Rick doesn't like it when people are lonely. We have home communities that meet all over town, and we consider this to be the heart of our church. Almost every church I have ever been to already does a great job at this.

Fourth: Authenticity. This is something of a buzzword, I know, but Imago actually lives this. I speak from the pulpit at Imago from time to time, and I am completely comfortable saying anything I like. I don't have to pretend to be godly in order for people to listen. Authenticity is an enormous value at Imago. I love this because by being true I am allowing people to get to know the real me, and it feels better to have people love the real me than the me I invented.

o   o   o

So one of the things I had to do after God provided a church for me was to let go of any bad attitude I had against the other churches I'd gone to. In the end, I was just different, you know. It wasn't that they were bad, they just didn't do it for me. I read through the book of Ephesians four times one night in Eugene Peterson's *The Message*, and it seemed to me that Paul did not want Christians to fight with one another. He seemed to care a great deal about this, so, in my mind, I had to tell my heart to love the people at the churches I used to go to, the people who were different from me. This was entirely freeing because when I told my heart to do this, my heart did it, and now I think very fondly of those wacko Republican fundamentalists, and I know that they love me, too, and I know that we will eat together, we will break bread together in heaven, and we will love each other so purely it will hurt because we are a family in Christ.

So here is a step-by-step formula for how you, too, can go to church without getting angry:

- Pray that God will show you a church filled with people who share your interests and values.

- Go to the church God shows you.

- Don't hold grudges against any other churches. God loves those churches almost as much as He loves yours.

13

Romance

Meeting Girls Is Easy

MY FRIEND KURT USED TO SAY FINDING A WIFE IS a percentage game. He said you have to have two or three relationships going at once, never letting the one girl know about the others, always "moving in to close the deal." One of them, he said, is bound to work out, and if you lose one, you just pick up another. Kurt believed you had to date about twenty girls before you found the one you were going to marry. He just believed it was easier to date them all at once. Kurt ended up marrying a girl from Dallas, and everybody says he married her for her money. He is very happy.

Elsewhere in the quandary is my friend Josh. When I first moved to Oregon I was befriended by this vibrant kid who read a lot of the Bible. Josh was good-looking and obsessed with dating, philosophies of dating, social rituals, and that sort of thing. He was homeschooled and raised to believe traditional dating was a bad idea. I traveled with him around the country and introduced him at seminars he would conduct on the pitfalls of dating. He wrote a book about it, and it hit the bestseller list. No kidding. A couple years later he moved to Baltimore and got married. I called him after the wedding and asked him how he got to know his wife without dating. He said they courted, which I understood to mean he had become Amish. But he explained courting is a lot like dating without the head games. He and his wife are also very happy.

My friend Mike Tucker reads books about dating and knows a lot on the subject. He says things like "You know, Don, relationships are like rubber bands . . . When one person pulls away, the other is attracted, and when the other person pulls away, well, that just draws the other one even closer." That sort of thing is interesting to a guy like me because I know nothing about dating. What little I know about dating is ridiculous and wouldn't help rabbits reproduce. I know you shouldn't make fun of a girl on a date and you shouldn't eat spaghetti. Other than these two things I am clueless.

Here's a tip I've never used: I understand you can learn a great deal about girldom by reading *Pride and Prejudice,* and I own a copy, but I have never read it. I tried. It was given to me by a girl with a little note inside that read: *What is in this book is the heart of a woman.* I am sure the heart of a woman is pure and lovely, but the first chapter of said heart is hopelessly boring. Nobody dies at all. I keep the book on my shelf because girls come into my room, sit on my couch, and eye the books on the adjacent shelf. You have a copy of *Pride and Prejudice,* they exclaim in a gentle sigh and smile. Yes, I say. Yes, I do.

o   o   o

Not long ago I went to Yosemite with my Canadian friend Julie. I have a weakness for Canadian girls. I don't know why, but when a Canadian girl asks me what I am thinking "aboat," I go nuts. So I have had this secret crush on Julie for a while, but she likes guys who surf and skateboard and jump out of airplanes with snowboards. I pretty much don't fit that description. I read books by dead guys. This is my identity. Besides, when Julie and I met I was in a relationship with a cute writer from the South, and Julie liked some other guy who could skateboard and play guitar. The thing with the writer didn't work out, however, because though we had everything in common we could not connect in the soul. So it happened that I was speaking in San Francisco and Julie was traveling around California and happened to be in a hostel in the city while I was there.

So I went to pick her up, and later we were driving through the Sierra Nevadas and I was nervous because she was much prettier than I remembered and we were making small talk about what we wanted in a mate, what we expected in marriage and that sort of thing. I kept wanting to say, Well, I want a tall Canadian girl who sings and plays the guitar, and is, um, not Alanis Morisette. But I couldn't say that because Julie would have been onto me. So I just told her I wanted a girl who would be a good mom, a girl who could go deep and meaningful with me spiritually, a girl who was good in bed. I said all the cliché stuff, the stuff that has been true for centuries. But then I opened my big stupid mouth and said that I thought, honestly, there really wasn't any such thing as true, true love. I was feeling tired when I said it. I don't know why I said it.

I kept talking with my stupid mouth. I told her that love, or what we call love, is mostly teamwork and that, quite possibly, I would get a crush on another woman after I had been married for a while. I also mentioned that my wife might become attracted to another man. The stuff that attracts us to other people doesn't shut down just because we walk down the aisle, I said. I was going on like this, being a realist and all, and I suspect I was saying stupid things like this because I have not read

Pride and Prejudice because it turns out these ideas are not the keys to a woman's heart. Julie believed that there was such a thing as true love and she would be in love with her mate forever and that he would be in love with her forever too.

Julie hated my ideas. She said nothing like that would ever happen to her, that her husband would love her passionately and adore her until one of them died. She did not really want to talk about my ideas. I just sat there feeling stupid. I do this a great deal in my life.

The next day, on the way to Santa Cruz, I told her I had a crush on her, which was stupid because I knew she didn't feel the same. I was only hoping she did. I did it very stupidly, very sheepishly. I just sort of stumbled around in my mouth, and my heart was beating very fast. Julie was very kind, but we sort of let it go and pretended the idea was never spoken. The rest of the time we made small talk and listened to Patty Griffin, which was helpful because Patty Griffin has always been very comforting to me.

I think if you like somebody you have to tell them. It might be embarrassing to say it, but you will never regret stepping up. I know from personal experience, however, that you should not keep telling a girl that you like her after she tells you she isn't into it. You should not keep riding your bike by her house either.

○   ○   ○

I don't want to get married right away. I think it will take me a while after I meet a girl. I like being single. I am one of the few who like it. I want to marry a girl who, when I am with her, makes me feel alone. I guess what I am saying is, I want to marry a girl whom I feel completely comfortable with, comfortable being myself. I can be very immature and awkward in moments, and I want to be able to be like that with her and not have her walk away or be embarrassed.

I've had about fifty people tell me that I fear intimacy. And it is true. I fear what people will think of me, and that is the reason I don't date very often. People really like me a lot when they only know me a little, but I have this great fear that if they knew me a lot they wouldn't like me. That is the number one thing that scares me about having a wife because she would have to know me pretty well in order to marry me and I think if she got to know me pretty well she wouldn't like me anymore.

My best friend, Paul, married my friend Danielle. People change when they get married, it is true. Danielle was a fiery feminist when she married Paul; now she isn't so much a feminist, or at least she isn't active. She is very much in love with him, and he with her. Sometimes, when I am visiting them, they grab each other's butts as if I am not even in the room. It's embarrassing. People shouldn't grab each other's butts with me sitting there in the room. Paul and Danielle have been married almost seven years and have three children, three girls. I was in the wedding. I read a poem. I look incredibly handsome and skinny in the pictures. Paul looked like Brad Pitt, and Danielle, who is hopelessly beautiful, looked like a flower or a beautiful painting.

For a while after the wedding, we all lived together in an enormous old house on Kearney Street in Portland. It was Wes and Maja's house, Danielle's aunt and uncle. The house once belonged to the Hall of Fame basketball player Bill Walton, and they say when Patty Hearst was kidnapped by the S.L.A., she was held captive in the basement. The old guy who lived next door said Walton used to have the Grateful Dead over and they would do concerts on the porch. On a dry day you can smell the marijuana residue in the woodwork.

It was an enormous house, and I lived in the attic. Paul and

Danielle lived in the grand room which was big enough to make into an apartment. Occasionally Paul would come up to the attic, and we would crawl out the window to the roof where we would smoke pipes above the city.

"How is married life?" I once asked.

"It's good. It's tough, but it is good."

"What is tough about it?" I asked.

Paul is the only person I know who is completely comfortable in his own skin, completely true in what he says. He is what they call a true person. "You know, Don, marriage is worth the trade. You lose all your freedom, but you get this friend. This incredible friend."

I wondered about that when he said it. The idea of marriage is remarkably frightening to me for precisely this reason: the loss of freedom. I am not somebody who needs constant company. I don't often get lonely. I live in community because it is healthy, because people who live alone for too long are more likely to go goofy, but the idea of coming home to a woman, day after day, living in the same house and sharing a bath and a bed and having things pink and silky lying around on the floor strikes this chord in me like a prison door clanging shut. I can just see myself standing there watching her take her makeup off in the bathroom and thinking, *She really isn't going to leave. All her stuff is here now.*

Tony the Beat Poet says I am finicky, that the longest I have been in love is eight minutes. That really isn't true. I just get crushes very quickly, like lightning or something, and then they go away. Mostly they go away because I am afraid to do anything about them. I am afraid of rejection, and I am afraid that I won't feel the same way tomorrow, and I have no faith in the system that God made.

Penny says I have a skewed view of relationships because I have issues with intimacy, and when I talk to Nadine about girls she just looks at me with her dignified stare, making knowing noises like a therapist. That's interesting, she says to me. Very interesting.

I know they all think I am selfish. And I am. I want a girl, but I want her every few days, not every day. I want her to have her own house and to come over only when I feel like shaving.

○   ○   ○

"It isn't what you think it is, Don." Paul takes his gaze from the city and eyes the pipe in his hand. He turns it over and taps the top ash onto the roof, rolling the embers under his sneakers.

"What isn't?"

"Marriage." He looks me in the eye. "It isn't fulfilling in the way you think it is."

"Paul, will you be honest with me if I ask you something?"

"Yes."

"Are you happy?"

"Define happy."

"Are you glad you married Danielle?"

Paul puts the stem of his pipe back in his mouth.

"I am happy, Don. I am very happy."

"What do you mean it isn't what I think it is then?" I was expecting him to talk about sex.

"Well, maybe I can't say what you think marriage is. Maybe I should say it isn't what I thought it would be. I thought to be married was to be known. And it is; it is to be known. But Danielle can only know me so much; do you know what I mean?"

"There are things you haven't told her?" I ask.

"I've told her everything."

"Then I don't know what you are saying."

Paul pushed himself up a little to the pitch of the roof from which you can see the Portland skyline. I joined him. "We all want to be loved, right?"

"Right."

"And the scary thing about relationships, intimate relationships, is that if somebody gets to know us, the us that we usually hide, they might not love us; they might reject us."

"Right," I tell him.

Paul continued. "I'm saying there is stuff I can't tell her, not because I don't want to, but because there aren't words. It's like we are separate people, and there is no getting inside each other to read each other's thoughts, each other's beings. Marriage is amazing because it is the closest two people can get, but they can't get all the way to that place of absolute knowing. Marriage is the most beautiful thing I have ever dreamed of, Don, but it isn't everything. It isn't Mecca. Danielle loves everything about me; she accepts me and tolerates me and encourages me. She knows me better than anybody else in the world, but she doesn't know all of me, and I don't know all of her. And I never thought after I got married there would still be something lacking. I always thought marriage, especially after I first met Danielle, would be the ultimate fulfillment. It is great, don't get me wrong, and I am glad I married Danielle, and I will be with her forever. But there are places in our lives that only God can go."

"So marriage isn't all that it is cracked up to be?" I ask.

"No, it is so much more than I ever thought it would be. One of the ways God shows me He loves me is through Danielle, and one of the ways God shows Danielle He loves her is through me. And because she loves me, and teaches me that I am lovable, I can better interact with God."

"What do you mean?"

"I mean that to be in a relationship with God is to be loved purely and furiously. And a person who thinks himself unlovable cannot be in a relationship with God because he can't accept who God is; a Being that is love. We learn that we are lovable or unlovable from other people," Paul says. "That is why God tells us so many times to love each other."

When the sky got dark Paul and I went back into the attic. We made small talk for an hour before he went downstairs to be with his wife, but I kept thinking about these things. I turned out the light and lay in my bed and thought about the girls I had dated, the fear I have of getting married, and the incredible selfishness from which I navigate my existence.

o   o   o

I had been working on a play called *Polaroids* that year. It was the story of one man's life from birth to death, each scene delivered through a monologue with other actors silently acting out parts behind the narrator as he walks the audience through his life journey. In the scene I had written a few nights before, I had the man fighting with his wife. They were experiencing unbearable tension after losing a son in a car accident the year before. I knew in my heart they were not going to make it, that *Polaroids* would include a painful divorce that showed the ugliness of separation. But I changed my mind. After talking with Paul I couldn't do it. I wondered what it would look like to have the couple stick it out. I got up and turned on my computer. I had the lead character in my play walk into the bedroom where his wife was sleeping. I had him kneel down by her and whisper some lines:

What great gravity is this that drew my soul toward yours? What great force, that though I went falsely, went kicking, went disguising myself to earn your love, also disguised, to earn your keeping, your resting, your staying, your will fleshed into mine, rasped by a slowly revealed truth, the barter of my soul, the soul that I fear, the soul that I loathe, the soul that: if you will love, I will love. I will redeem you, if you will redeem me? Is this our purpose, you and I together to pacify each other, to lead each other toward the lie that we are good, that we are noble, that we need not redemption, save the one that you and I invented of our own clay?

I am not scared of you, my love, I am scared of me.

I went looking, I wrote out a list, I drew an image, I bled a poem of you. You were pretty, and my friends believed I was worthy of you. You were clever, but I was smarter, perhaps the only one smarter, the only one able to lead you. You see, love, I did not love you, I loved me. And you were only a tool that I used to fix myself, to fool myself, to redeem myself. And though I have taught you to lay your lily hand in mine, I walk alone, for I cannot talk to you, lest you talk it back to me, lest I believe that I am not worthy, not deserving, not redeemed.

I want desperately for you to be my friend. But you are not my friend; you have slid up warmly to the man I wanted to be, the man I pretended to be, and I was your Jesus and, you were mine. Should I show you who I am, we may crumble. I am not scared of you, my love, I am scared of me.

I want to be known and loved anyway. Can you do this? I trust by your easy breathing that you are human like me, that you are fallen like me, that you are lonely, like me. My love, do I know you? What is this great gravity that pulls us so painfully toward each other? Why do we not connect? Will we be forever in fleshing this out? And how will we with words, narrow words, come into the knowing of each other? Is this God's way of meriting grace, of teaching us of the labyrinth of His love for us, teaching us, in degrees, that which He is sacrificing to join ourselves to Him? Or better yet, has He formed our being fractional so that we might conclude one great hope, plodding and sighing and breathing into one another in such a great push that we might break through into the known and being loved, only to cave into a greater perdition and fall down at His throne still begging for our acceptance? Begging for our completion?

We were fools to believe that we would redeem each other.

Were I some sleeping Adam, to wake and find you resting at my rib, to share these things that God has done, to walk you through the garden, to counsel your timid steps, your bewildered eye, your heart so slow to love, so careful to love, so sheepish that I stepped up my aim and became a man. Is this what God intended? That though He made you from my rib, it is you who is making me, humbling me, destroying me, and in so doing revealing Him.

Will we be in ashes before we are one?

What great gravity is this that drew my heart toward yours? What great force collapsed my orbit, my lonesome state? What is this that wants in me the want in you? Don't we go at each other with yielded eyes, with cumbered hands and feet, with clunky tongues? This deed is unattainable! We cannot know each other!

I am quitting this thing, but not what you think. I am not going away.

I will give you this, my love, and I will not bargain or barter any longer. I will love you, as sure as He has loved me. I will discover what I can discover and though you remain a mystery, save God's own knowledge, what I disclose of you I will keep in the warmest chamber of my heart, the very chamber where God has stowed Himself in me. And I will do this to my death, and to death it may bring me.

I will love you like God, because of God, mighted by the power of God. I will stop expecting your love, demanding your love, trading for your love, gaming for your love. I will simply love. I am giving myself to you, and tomorrow I will do it again. I suppose the clock itself will wear thin its time before I am ended at this altar of dying and dying again.

God risked Himself on me. I will risk myself on you. And together, we will learn to love, and perhaps then, and only then, understand this gravity that drew Him, unto us.

14

Alone

Fifty-three Years in Space

I WAS IN LOVE ONCE. I THINK LOVE IS A BIT OF heaven. When I was in love I thought about that girl so much I felt like I was going to die and it was beautiful, and she loved me, too, or at least she said she did, and we were not about ourselves, we were about each other, and that is what I mean when I say being in love is a bit of heaven. When I was in love I hardly thought of myself; I thought of her and how beautiful she looked and whether or not she was cold and how I could make her laugh. It was wonderful because I forgot my problems. I owned her problems instead, and her problems seemed romantic and beautiful. When I was in love there was somebody in the world who was more important than me, and that, given all that happened at the fall of man, is a miracle, like something God forgot to curse.

I no longer think being in love is the polar opposite of being alone, however. I say that because I used to want to be in love again as I assumed this was the opposite of loneliness. I think being in love is an opposite of loneliness, but not the opposite. There are other things I now crave when I am lonely, like community, like friendship, like family. I think our society puts too much pressure on romantic love, and that is why so many romances fail. Romance can't possibly carry all that we want it to.

Tony the Beat Poet says the words *alone, lonely,* and *loneliness* are three of the most powerful words in the English language. I agree with Tony. Those words say that we are human; they are like the words *hunger* and *thirst.* But they are not words about the body, they are words about the soul.

I am something of a recluse by nature. I am that cordless screwdriver that has to charge for twenty hours to earn ten minutes use. I need that much downtime. I am a terrible daydreamer. I have been since I was a boy. My mind goes walking and playing and skipping. I invent characters, write stories, pretend I am a rock star, pretend I am a legendary poet, pretend I am an astronaut, and there is no control to my mind.

When you live on your own for a long time, however, your personality changes because you go so much into yourself you lose the ability to be social, to understand what is and isn't normal behavior. There is an entire world inside yourself, and if you let yourself, you can get so deep inside it you will forget the way to the surface. Other people keep our souls alive, just like food and water does with our body.

A few years back some friends and I hiked to Jefferson Park, high on the Pacific Crest Trail at the base of Mount Jefferson. One evening we were sitting around a campfire telling stories when we spotted a ranger slowly walking toward our camp. He was a small man, thin, but he moved slowly as though he was tired. He ascended the small slope toward our fire by pushing his hands against his knees. When he met us he did not introduce himself, he only gazed into the fire for a while. We addressed him, and he nodded. He kindly asked to see our permits. We went to our tents and to our backpacks and brought the permits to him unfolded. He studied each of them slowly, staring at the documents as if he had slipped into a daydream. They were simple documents, really, just green slips of paper with a signature. But he eyed them like moving pictures, like cartoons. Eventually he handed our permits back to us, smiling, nodding, looking awfully queer. And then he stood there. He leaned against a tree only two feet from our campfire and watched us. We asked him a few questions, asked him if he needed anything else, but he kindly said no. Finally, I figured it out.

He was lonely. He was alone and going nuts.

He had forgotten how to engage people. I asked him how long he had been at Jeff Park. Two months, he said. Two months, I asked, all by yourself? Yeah, he said and smiled. That's a long time to be alone, I told him. Well, he said to me, this conversation has worn me out. He put his hands in his pockets and smiled again. He looked out into the distance and stretched his neck to look at the stars.

"Do believe I will head back to camp," he said. He didn't say good-bye. He walked down the little hill and into the darkness.

o　　o　　o

I know about that feeling, that feeling of walking out into the darkness. When I lived alone it was very hard for me to be around people. I would leave parties early. I would leave church before worship was over so I didn't have to stand around and talk. The presence of people would agitate me. I was so used to being able to daydream and keep myself company that other people were an intrusion. It was terribly unhealthy.

o　　o　　o

My friend Mike Tucker loves people. He says if he isn't around people for a long time he starts to lose it, starts to talk to himself, making up stories. Before he moved to Portland he was a long-haul trucker, which is a no-good job for a guy who doesn't do well alone. He said one time, on a trip from Los Angeles to Boston, he had a three-hour conversation with Abraham Lincoln. He said it was amazing. I bet it was, I told him. Tuck said Mr. Lincoln was very humble and brilliant and best of all a good listener.

Tuck said prostitutes would hang out at truck stops, going from truck to truck asking the guys if they needed company. He said one night he got so lonely he almost asked a girl to come in. He didn't even want to have sex. He just wanted a girl to hold him, wanted somebody with skin on, somebody who would listen and talk back with a real voice when he asked a question.

Sometimes when I go to bed at night or when I first wake up in the morning, I talk to my pillow as if it were a woman, a make-believe wife. I tell her I love her and that she's a beautiful wife and all. I don't know if I do this because I am lonely or not. Tuck says I do this because I am horny. He says loneliness is real painful, and I will know it when I feel it. I think it is interesting that God designed people to need other people. We see those cigarette advertisements with the rugged cowboy riding around alone on a horse, and we think that is strength, when, really, it is like setting your soul down on a couch and not exercising it. The soul needs to interact with other people to be healthy.

o o o

A long time ago I was holed up in an apartment outside Portland. I was living with a friend, but he had a girlfriend across town and was spending his time with her, even his nights. I didn't have a television. I ate by myself and washed clothes by myself and didn't bother keeping the place clean because I didn't know anybody who would be coming by. I would talk to myself sometimes, my voice coming back funny off the walls and the ceiling. I would play records and pretend I was the singer. I did a great Elvis. I would read the poetry of Emily Dickinson out loud and pretend to have conversations with her. I asked her what she meant by "zero at the bone," and I asked her if she was a lesbian. For the record, she told me she wasn't a lesbian. She was sort of offended by the question, to be honest. Emily Dickinson was the most interesting person I'd ever met. She was lovely, really, sort of quiet like a scared dog, but she engaged fine when she warmed up to me. She was terribly brilliant.

I had been living in that apartment for two years when I decided to cross the country to visit Amherst, Massachusetts, where Emily lived and died. Back then I imagined her as the perfect woman, so quietly brilliant all those years, wrapping her poems neatly in bundles of paper and rope. I confess I daydreamed about living in her Amherst, in her century, befriending her during her days at Holyoke Seminary, walking with her through those summer hills she spoke so wonderfully of, the hills that, in the morning, untied their bonnets. My friend Laura at Reed tells me that half the guys she knows have had crushes on Emily Dickinson. She says it is because Emily was brilliant and yet not threatening, having lived under the thumb of her father so long. She thinks the reason guys get crushes on Emily Dickinson is because Emily is an intellectual submissive, and intellectual men fear the domination of women. I don't care why we get crushes on Emily Dickinson. It is a rite of passage for any thinking man. Any thinking American man.

I only tell you all of this to show you how bad it gets when you aren't around real people for a long time. I tell you of Emily

Dickinson because she reminds me of the first time I thought, perhaps, I had lost my mind in isolation. I know now it was an apparition of loneliness, but I cannot tell you how very real it seemed that evening in Amherst. The other times I had seen her it was all invention; I was creating her out of boredom. But this was different.

I had driven from New York City to Boston the night before and had slept in my car. I stopped in Boston because I was too tired to drive the night. I was so cold under a towel I turned and rubbed against a seat belt that knotted itself in my back and against the handle of the door that crowded my head. I lay there in the backseat and stared at the roof of the car, thinking about Emily Dickinson. I hardly got any sleep. In the morning I doped up on coffee and started on the last leg of my journey, the leg that led to Amherst.

o   o   o

All the pretty girls at UMASS were running in their sweats that afternoon, the kids out smoking on the lawn, the trees behind them just sticks of things, just cobalt sky out for a walk. The place is lovely in the winter, very smart feeling, very bookish. The big houses are not close together. Red brick and ivy. Long lawns.

Across town from UMASS is Amherst College. Emily's grandfather started Amherst College because he wanted women to know the Bible as well as men. He was all vision and no hands, it seemed, and the place went bankrupt nearly immediately. The school was saved years later by the man's son, Emily's father, who was not like her grandfather in that he did not believe in the freedom or equality of women. Emily's father kept women down. Austin, Emily's brother, not Emily, was expected by the family to publish, to be a great writer.

I was thinking about these things when I circled Amherst College and stopped at the Jones Library where some handwritten notes from Emily are kept, scribbles mostly, gentle pencil on a yellowed sheet within a glass case. It was like magic looking at them. I felt ashamed because I knew I had been reading her for only a year, and yet I felt as though I knew her, as though we were dear friends, what with her living in the apartment in Oregon with me and all.

The man at Jones Library told me where to find the homestead, not much of a place, he said, and indeed I had passed it on the way into town without knowing it. I thought I would have felt it in my chest or sensed it to my right. I thought it would have been largely marked. I followed the man's instructions and walked from the library down along the shops back toward Boston a mile. Her house is not very much like what you would think. Though it is big it is not grand, and there is a large tree in front that takes the view. A side door is greeted by concrete steps, the cheap sort, and the driveway has been paved. There is a historical marker, but it is small, and so the first thing a young man realizes when he visits the home of Emily Dickinson is that the world is, in fact, not as in love with her as he is. I wanted to gather the leaves, you know, clean up the place. And I was looking all about the house, before making my approach, when I saw this thing that was not her but only in my mind was her, swing open the side door and set a foot quickly on the step. She met my eyes and went white, whiter than she already was, anyway, and like a wind she fled back into the house. The door closed as if it were on a spring. For a second I could not move.

I wrote in my journal that evening:

"I saw Emily Dickinson step out of a screen door and look at me with dark eyes, those endless dark eyes like the mouth of a cave, like pitch night set so lovely twice beneath her furrowed brow, her pale white skin gathering at the red of her lips, her long thin neck coming perfectly from her white dress flowing so gently and clean around her waist, down around her knees then slipping a tickle across her ankles. And then she went back into the house and it scared me to walk around the place."

Penny says it is when they are in their twenties that people lose their minds. She says this is what happened to her mother. And when we talk about it, I think of myself in Amherst, so confident at the thing I saw, and at once confident there was nothing there because Emily is dead.

I stopped imagining her immediately. I never told anybody about this because nothing like this happened anymore, so there was no need, and what's more I couldn't bear to find out that I was going crazy, that I was indeed seeing things. I blamed it on loneliness of the biochemical sort. When a person has no other persons he invents them because he was not designed to be alone, because it isn't good for a person to be alone.

There once was a man named
Don Astronaut.

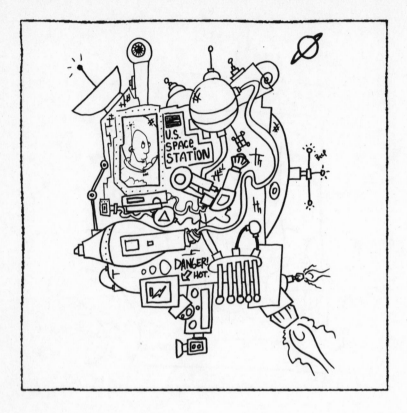

Don Astronaut lived on
a space station out in space.

Don Astronaut had
a special space suit that kept
him alive without food or
water or oxygen.

One day there was an accident.

And Don Astronaut was
cast out into space.

Don Astronaut orbited the earth
and was very scared.

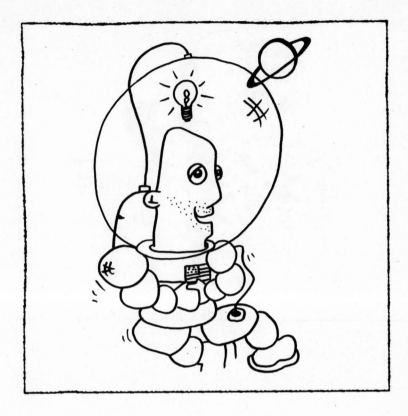

Until he remembered his special
suit that kept him alive.

But nobody's government came
to rescue Don Astronaut because
it would cost too much money.
(There was a conspiracy, and they
said he had died, but he hadn't.)

So Don Astronaut
orbited the earth again
and again, fourteen
times each day.

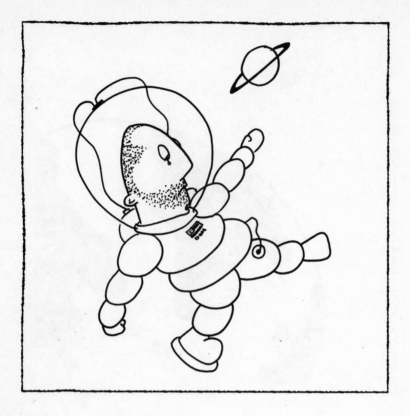

And Don Astronaut orbited
the earth for months.

And Don Astronaut orbited
the earth for decades.

And Don Astronaut orbited the earth
for fifty-three years before he died a
very lonely and crazy man—just a shell of
a thing with hardly a spark for a soul.

One of my new housemates, Stacy, wants to write a story about an astronaut. In his story the astronaut is wearing a suit that keeps him alive by recycling his fluids. In the story the astronaut is working on a space station when an accident takes place, and he is cast into space to orbit the earth, to spend the rest of his life circling the globe. Stacy says this story is how he imagines hell, a place where a person is completely alone, without others and without God. After Stacy told me about his story, I kept seeing it in my mind. I thought about it before I went to sleep at night. I imagined myself looking out my little bubble helmet at blue earth, reaching toward it, closing it between my puffy white space-suit fingers, wondering if my friends were still there. In my imagination I would call to them, yell for them, but the sound would only come back loud within my helmet. Through the years my hair would grow long in my helmet and gather around my forehead and fall across my eyes. Because of my helmet I would not be able to touch my face with my hands to move my hair out of my eyes, so my view of earth, slowly, over the first two years, would dim to only a thin light through a curtain of thatch and beard.

I would lay there in bed thinking about Stacy's story, putting myself out there in the black. And there came a time, in space, when I could not tell whether I was awake or asleep. All my thoughts mingled together because I had no people to remind me what was real and what was not real. I would punch myself in the side to feel pain, and this way I could be relatively sure I was not dreaming. Within ten years I was beginning to breathe heavy through my hair and my beard as they were pressing tough against my face and had begun to curl into my mouth and up my nose. In space, I forgot that I was human. I did not know whether I was a ghost or an apparition or a demon thing.

After I thought about Stacy's story, I lay there in bed and wanted to be touched, wanted to be talked to. I had the terrifying thought that something like that might happen to me. I thought it was just a terrible story, a painful and ugly story. Stacy had delivered as accurate a description of a hell as could be calculated. And what is sad, what is very sad, is that we are proud people, and because we have sensitive egos and so many of us live our lives in front of our televisions, not having to deal with real people who might hurt us or offend us, we float along on our couches like astronauts moving aimlessly through the Milky Way, hardly interacting with other human beings at all.

○ ○ ○

Stacy's story frightened me badly so I called Penny. Penny is who I call when I am thinking too much. She knows about this sort of thing. It was late, but I asked her if I could come over. She said yes. I took the bus from Laurelhurst, and there were only a few people on the bus, and none of them were talking to each other. When I got to Reed, Penny greeted me with a hug and a kiss on the cheek. We hung out in her room for a while and made small talk. It was so nice to hear another human voice. She had a picture of her father on her desk, tall and thin and wearing a cowboy hat. She told me about her father and how, when she was a child, she and her sister Posie spent a year sailing in the Pacific. She said they were very close. I listened so hard because it felt like, while she was telling me stories, she was massaging my soul, letting me know I was not alone, that I will never have to be alone, that there are friends and family and churches and coffee shops. I was not going to be cast into space.

We left the dorms and walked across Blue Bridge, a beautiful walking bridge on the campus at Reed that stretches across a canyon, fit with blue lights, which, when you look at them with blurred eyes, feels like stars lighting a path winding toward heaven.

The air was very cold, but Penny and I sat outside commons and smoked pipes, and she asked me about my family and asked me what I dreamed and asked me how I felt about God.

Loneliness is something that happens to us, but I think it is something we can move ourselves out of. I think a person who is lonely should dig into a community, give himself to a community, humble himself before his friends, initiate community, teach people to care for each other, love each other. Jesus does not want us floating through space or sitting in front of our televisions. Jesus wants us interacting, eating together, laughing together, praying together. Loneliness is something that came with the fall.

If loving other people is a bit of heaven then certainly isolation is a bit of hell, and to that degree, here on earth, we decide in which state we would like to live.

Rick told me, a little later, I should be living in community. He said I should have people around bugging me and getting under my skin because without people I could not grow—I could not grow in God, and I could not grow as a human. We are born into families, he said, and we are needy at first as children because God wants us together, living among one another, not hiding ourselves under logs like fungus. You are not a fungus, he told me, you are a human, and you need other people in your life in order to be healthy.

Rick told me there was a group of guys at the church looking to get a house, looking to live in community. He told me I should consider joining them.

Community

Living with Freaks

BEFORE I LIVED IN COMMUNITY, I THOUGHT FAITH, mine being Christian faith, was something a person did alone, like monks in caves. I thought the backbone of faith was time alone with God, time reading ancient texts and meditating on poetry or the precepts of natural law and, perhaps, when a person gets good and godly, levitating potted plants or pitchers of water.

It seems that way in books. I had read a Christian book about the betterment of self, the actualization of the individual in the personal journey toward God. The book was all about focus and drive and perspective. It was all stuff you did in a quiet room. None of it had anything to do with community.

If other people were a part of the Christian journey, they had small roles; they were accountability partners or counselors or husbands or wives. I hadn't seen a single book (outside the majority of books in the New Testament) that addressed a group of people or a community with advice about faith.

When I walked into the Christian section of a bookstore, the message was clear: Faith is something you do alone.

Rick does not have much tolerance for people living alone.

He's like Bill Clinton in that he feels everyone's pain. If Rick thinks somebody is lonely, he can't sleep at night. He wants us all to live with each other and play nice so he can get some rest. Tortured soul.

I didn't know what to think about the idea of living in community at first. I had lived on my own for about six years, and the idea of moving in with a bunch of slobs didn't appeal to me. Living in community sounded so, um, odd. Cults do that sort of thing, you know. First you live in community, and then you drink punch and die.

It was Rick's idea, though, and he seemed fairly normal in all the other areas of his life. He never mentioned anything about a spaceship trailing behind a comet. He never asked us to store weapons or peanut butter, so I figured the thing about living in community was on the up-and-up. Just because something looks like a cult doesn't mean it really is, right? The other thing is that, at the time, I was pushing thirty and still not married. When you are thirty and not married and you move in with a bunch of guys, you look like you have given up, like you are a bunch of losers who live together so you can talk about computers and share video games.

If I lived in community, we would have to have about five raging parties just to shake the loser image. But I am not one to party. I like going to bed at nine and watching CNN till I fall asleep. So I was thinking I could move in with the guys and we could tell everybody we had raging parties but never actually have them.

I didn't know whether to make the move or not.

Rick kept bothering me about it. I was living way out in the country, about thirty miles from town, and he kept asking me if I was lonely out there, if I wouldn't much rather move into town with a bunch of guys from the church. He asked if I had the chance to minister to anybody out there in the country. He asked if I was having any influence on the cows. I told him I was having a lot of influence. I wrote books. He laughed. I sat there uncomfortably while he laughed. "Books," he said. "Brilliant! You write books for people." He couldn't stop laughing. He was being very annoying.

o   o   o

I moved in with five other guys about a month after talking with Rick. We found a house in Laurelhurst, one of the houses on the traffic circle at 39th and Glisan. We lived across the street from the giant statue of Joan of Arc. You'll see the statue if you come to Portland.

I liked it at first. It was a big house, and I got the best room, the room with all the windows. My room literally had windows on every wall, about ten windows in all. It was like living in a green house. I set my desk in front of the huge window that looked down on the traffic circle and the statue. My friends used to drive around the circle and honk when they went by. I always forgot I lived in a glass room so I would pull my finger out of my nose just in time to wave back. I went from living in complete isolation to living in a glass box on a busy street.

One of the best things about living in community was that I had brothers for the first time ever. We used to sit on the porch and watch cars go around the roundabout. We used to stare at the statue of Joan of Arc and wonder, out loud, if we could take her in a fight.

I have a picture on my desk of the six guys at Graceland, which is what we named the house. People thought we named the house Graceland because we wanted it to be a place where people experienced God's grace and unconditional love. But we didn't think about that till later. We really named it Graceland because that was the name of the house Elvis lived in, and, like Elvis, we were all pretty good with the ladies.

The picture on my desk is more than a picture of six guys; it is a picture of me in my transition, not a physical transition but more of an inner shift from one sort of thinking to another. I don't look all that tired in the picture, but I remember being tired. I remember feeling tired for almost a year. I was tired because I wasn't used to being around people all the time.

The picture was taken on the porch. We were all smoking pipes. I was wearing a black stocking cap, like a beat poet or a bank robber. Andrew the Protester, the tall good-looking one with dark hair and the beard, the one who looks like a young Fidel Castro, was the activist in our bachelor family. He is the guy I told you about with whom I go to protests. He works with the homeless downtown and is studying at Portland State to become a social worker. He is always talking about how outrageous the Republicans are or how wrong it is to eat beef. I honestly don't know how Andrew got so tall without eating beef.

Jeremy, the guy in the Wranglers with the marine haircut, is the cowboy in the family. He always carries a gun. You'd think Andrew and Jeremy would hate each other because Andrew opposes the right to bear arms, but they get along okay, good-natured guys and all. It is a shame because that would be a great fight. Jeremy wants to be a cop, and he went to college on a wrestling scholarship, and Andrew is a communist. I would try to get them to fight, but they liked each other.

Mike Tucker, whom we all refer to as Tuck, was the older brother in the clan, the responsible one. He is the one with the spiked red hair, like Richie Cunningham fused with a rock star. Mike was a trucker for years but always dreamed of a career in advertising. He moved to Portland and started his own advertising agency with just a cell phone and a Web site. He posed nude on his brochure, which got him gigs with Doc Martens and a local fashion agency. He freelances every other day and drives trucks the rest of the time. Mike is one of my best friends in the world. Mike is one of the greatest guys I know.

Simon, the short good-looking guy with the black hair and sly grin, was the leprechaun of our tribe. He's a deeply spiritual Irishman here for the year from Dublin. Simon is a womanizer, always heading down to Kell's for a pint with the lads or to the church to pray and ask God's forgiveness for his detestable sins and temper. Simon came to America on a J-1 visa. He came to Portland, specifically, to study our church. He wants to go back to the homeland and start a Christian revival, returning the country to its faith in Jesus, the living God. After that, he wants to unite men and take England captive, forcing them to be slaves to the Irish, the greatest of all peoples, the people who invented honor, integrity, Western civilization, Guinness and, apparently, peanut butter and the light bulb.

Trevor, the young guy in the picture, looks like Justin Timberlake, like the lead singer of a boy band. He has tight hair that curls just out of the shoot, and he's died it blond. Trev is the kid, the rookie on our team of misfits. He is just out of high school a few years and rides a Yamaha crotch-rocket motorcycle so fast that when he lets me drive it, I can hardly keep the front wheel on the ground. He is a learner, with a solid heart like a sponge that absorbs, and he wants to become a very good man. Trevor is one of my favorite people. He is my Nintendo buddy. We yell profanities at each other while playing NFL Blitz. I usually win because he is slow with the fingers. Sometimes, after I beat him in the game, he crawls into his little bed and cries himself to sleep. After that I usually feel sorry for him, and I let him win a game or two. Rookie.

○   ○   ○

I liked them all very much, but we had hard times. I was a serious recluse before I moved in with the guys at Graceland. When you live on your own for years, you begin to think the world belongs to you. You begin to think all space is your space and all time is your time.

It is like in that movie *About a Boy* where Nick Hornby's chief character, played by Hugh Grant, believes that life is a play about himself, that all other characters are only acting minor roles in a story that centers around him. My life felt like that. Life was a story about me because I was in every scene. In fact, I was the only one in every scene. I was everywhere I went. If somebody walked into my scene, it would frustrate me because they were disrupting the general theme of the play, namely my comfort or glory. Other people were flat characters in my movie, lifeless characters. Sometimes I would have scenes with them, dialogue, and they would speak their lines, and I would speak mine. But the movie, the grand movie stretching from Adam to the Antichrist, was about me. I wouldn't have told you that at the time, but that is the way I lived.

Tuck was one of my best friends when he moved in. He is still one of my best friends, but for a while I wanted to kill him. He did not understand that life was a movie about me. Nobody ever told him. He would knock on my door while I was reading, come in and sit down in a chair opposite me, and then he would want to talk, he would want to hear about my day. I couldn't believe it. The audacity to come into my room, my soundstage, and interrupt the obvious flow of the story with questions about how I am.

I would give Tuck little signals that I didn't want to talk like eye rolls or short answers to his questions. I would stare into space so he thought I was crazy or snore so he would think I had fallen asleep. I think I hurt his feelings. He would get very frustrated with me, go upstairs, and wonder why I was acting that way. He only did this a few times before he dismissed me as a jerk. I almost lost the friendship, to be honest.

I didn't like the feeling of having to work with people. We would have a community meeting and talk about who wasn't doing their chores or who was leaving dirty dishes in the sink, and if I felt accused I would lash back at whoever accused me. I was confident I was right and they were wrong. I could not see, at the time, that I was being rude. There were a few times when Trevor actually stood up and walked out of the room. It was always because of me. The other guys had lived with people before. They knew all about people.

Living in community made me realize one of my faults: I was addicted to myself. All I thought about was myself. The only thing I really cared about was myself. I had very little concept of love, altruism, or sacrifice. I discovered that my mind is like a radio that picks up only one station, the one that plays me: *K-DON, all Don, all the time.*

I did not understand the exchange that takes place in meaningful dialogue, when two people sit down and tune their radios, if only for a moment, to the other person's station. It must have been painful for Tuck to try so desperately to catch my station, and for me to brush him off.

Having had my way for so long, I became defensive about what I perceived as encroachments on my rights. My personal bubble was huge. I couldn't have conversations that lasted more than ten minutes. I wanted efficiency in personal interaction, and while listening to one of my housemates talk, I wondered why they couldn't get to the point. *What are you trying to tell me?* I would think. *Do we really have to stand here and make small talk?*

Tuck told me later that in the first few months of living with me he felt judged, as though there was something wrong with him. He felt unvalued any time he was around me.

o   o   o

The most difficult lie I have ever contended with is this: Life is a story about me.

o   o   o

God brought me to Graceland to rid me of this deception, to scrub it out of the gray matter of my mind. It was a frustrating and painful experience.

I hear addicts talk about the shakes and panic attacks and the highs and lows of resisting their habit, and to some degree I understand them because I have had habits of my own, but no drug is so powerful as the drug of self. No rut in the mind is so deep as the one that says I am the world, the world belongs to me, all people are characters in my play. There is no addiction so powerful as self-addiction.

o   o   o

In the spring of my year at Graceland, when the ground was beginning to dry at Laurelhurst Park, a friend and I traveled to Salem to hear Brennan Manning speak. Manning is a former Catholic priest and a wonderful writer who has struggled with alcoholism and speaks frankly about matters of Christian spirituality.

We sat so close I could see the blue in Brennan's eyes and that quality of sincerity you find in people who have turned trial into service. Brennan grew up in New York and speaks with a slight East Coast bite that has been sanded down by years of smoking.

An ear has to work a bit to keep his pace. He opened his talk with the story of Zacchaeus. Brennan talked about how an entire town, with their ridicule and hatred, could not keep the little man from oppressing them through the extravagant financial gains he made as a tax collector. Christ walked through town, Brennan said, and spotted the man. Christ told Zacchaeus that He would like to have a meal with him.

In the single conversation Christ had with Zacchaeus, Brennan reminded us, Jesus spoke affirmation and love, and the tax collector sold his possessions and made amends to those he had robbed. It was the affection of Christ, not the brutality of a town, that healed Zacchaeus.

Manning went on to speak of the great danger of a harsh word, the power of unlove to deteriorate a person's heart and spirit, and how, as representatives of the grace and love of God, our communication should be seasoned with love and compassion.

While Manning was speaking, I was being shown myself, and I felt like God was asking me to change. I was being asked to walk away from the lies I believed about the world being about me. I had been communicating unlove to my housemates because I thought they were not cooperating with the meaning of life, that meaning being my desire and will and choice and comfort.

There was nothing fun about going home that night. I went with new eyes, seeing my housemates as people. For the first time I saw them as people, and I could sense God's love for them. I had been living with God's prized possessions, His children, the dear ones to Him, and had considered them a bother to this earth that was mine, this space and time that were mine.

o   o   o

In the short year at Graceland I hurt all the guys at one time or another. Fixing the carnage would take time. I had to make things right with each of them. I had really messed things up. Jeremy, the guy with the marine haircut who was going to become a cop, couldn't stand me. I had run my car through the garage door one night and neglected to fix it. Jeremy parked his motorcycle in the garage and so he had to use the broken door every day. My room was directly above the garage, so when Jeremy went to work in the morning at five o'clock, he would start his motorcycle engine, and it sounded like somebody was starting a lawn mower next to my bed. I would get furious, and later that night I would ask him if there was something we could do. He said no, that was where he needed to keep his motorcycle. And that was true. So, every time Jeremy had trouble getting the broken door up and down, he would get mad at me, and every time he started his motorcycle at 5:00 A.M., I would get mad at him. The issue, of course, was not about the motorcycle or the door; the issue was about whether or not we respected each other, whether or not we liked each other.

One evening I was down in the basement talking to Tuck while he was working out. I decided to do some laundry while I was down there, but somebody's clothes were in the dryer. There was no place to put them so I put them on the floor. I didn't think anything of it, you know, because the floor was pretty clean, but it turned out the clothes were Jeremy's and, later that night, when he got home, he wrote a note on our white board to the person who had thrown his clothes on the floor. I didn't actually throw them on the floor, I just sort of set them there, but still, he was pretty heated. I told him it was me, and I apologized. He had to go for a walk he was so mad. It was the last straw for him.

When he came back I asked him if we could talk. I told him it was time we dealt with it. He kept wanting to walk away from the conversation because he was so mad, but I wouldn't let him. I was ready to apologize. I told him I didn't feel like he cared about me because he started his motorcycle every morning, and I had become defensive about that, and that made me want to get him back, and I had done that sort of subconsciously, with little comments and that sort of thing. I had never told him, at the very beginning, that I felt like he didn't like me and I wanted him to. Instead, I had been proud and passive-aggressive. That was why we were experiencing all of this. And I told him that I felt bad. I didn't accuse him of anything, which looking back was very, very important. And, also, I didn't expect anything from him in return. I really didn't feel like he owed me anything. Jeremy listened very carefully once he had calmed down. He was great. He told me how much he liked me, and that meant the world to me. In that moment I could feel all the anger I had been feeling melt away. I couldn't even remember what I was angry about. And the next morning, when Jeremy started his motorcycle, it didn't even wake me up.

I was in San Francisco recently staying at this bed and breakfast place for people who are in the city to do ministry. It was a small house, but there were probably fifteen people living there at the time. The guy who ran the place, Bill, was always making meals or cleaning up after us, and I took note of his incredible patience and kindness. I noticed that not all of us did our dishes after a meal, and very few people thanked him for cooking. One morning, before anybody woke up, Bill and I were drinking coffee at the dining room table. I told him I lived with five guys and that it was very difficult for me because I liked my space and needed my privacy. I asked him how he kept such a good attitude all of the time with so many people abusing his kindness. Bill set down his coffee and looked me in the eye. "Don," he said. "If we are not willing to wake up in the morning and die to ourselves, perhaps we should ask ourselves whether or not we are really following Jesus."

16

Money

Thoughts on Paying Rent

WRITERS DON'T MAKE ANY MONEY AT ALL. WE MAKE about a dollar. It is terrible. But then again we don't work either. We sit around in our underwear until noon then go downstairs and make coffee, fry some eggs, read the paper, read part of a book, smell the book, wonder if perhaps we ourselves should work on our book, smell the book again, throw the book across the room because we are quite jealous that any other person wrote a book, feel terribly guilty about throwing the schmuck's book across the room because we secretly wonder if God in heaven noticed our evil jealousy, or worse, our laziness. We then lie across the couch facedown and mumble to God to forgive us because we are secretly afraid He is going to dry up all our words because we envied another man's stupid words. And for this, as I said before, we are paid a dollar. We are worth so much more.

I hate not having money. I hate not being able to go to a movie or out for coffee. I hate that feeling at the ATM when, after getting cash, the little receipt spits out, the one with the number on it, the telling number, the ever low number that translates into how many days I have left to feel comfortable.

The ATM, to me, often feels like a slot machine. I walk up to it hoping to get lucky.

I feel like a complete loser when I don't have money. That's the real problem. I feel invalidated, as if the gods have not approved my existence, as if my allowance has been cut off. We are worth our earning potential, you know. We are worth the money we make. Maybe this is a man thing; maybe women don't think about this, I don't know, but I think about it. I think I am worth what I earn, which makes me worth one dollar. Not having money affects the way a man thinks about himself. Last year I didn't have any money at all. Five of twelve months last year I prayed God would send me rent. Five of twelve months I received a check in the mail the day rent was due. I was grateful at first, but after a while, to be honest with you, I began to feel like God's charity. At the end of each month I would start biting my nails, wondering what account owed me money or whether or not I would pick up any writing assignments. There's not a lot of work in the Christian market if you won't write self-righteous, conservative propaganda. I write new-realism essays. I am not a commodity.

I wondered whether or not I was lazy. When you are a writer you feel lazy even when you're working. Who gets paid to sit around in a coffee shop all day and type into a computer? But I did work, I kept telling myself. I showed up at Palio every day, and in the evenings I would go to Common Ground. I worked. I wrote. I drove myself crazy writing.

The thing is, at the time, I was writing without a contract. So I wasn't really writing for money, I was writing in hopes of money. And when you are writing without a contract, you feel as though everything you say is completely worthless (technically it is, until you get a contract).

You can write all day and still not feel that you have done

anything. A man needs to do some work, needs to get his hands dirty and calloused and needs to hammer his thumb every once in a while. He needs to get tired at the end of the day, and not just mind tired, body tired too.

I wasn't feeling body tired, I was just feeling mind tired, and I didn't have any money, so I wasn't feeling like a man. I was in a bad place.

I talked to Rick about it. He came over to the house, and we were sitting around, and I asked him if he thought God really called me to be a writer or if I was just being lazy, being selfish, tinkering with words. He asked me if I worked; he said that everybody needs to work. I told him I did but wasn't getting paid for it because I didn't have a contract yet, and getting a contract was no sure thing. At best I was gambling. He said he didn't know whether what I was doing was right or wrong. He said he would pray for me. I rolled my eyes. He told me I had a gift and he liked me, and God would make things clear if I was being a lazy slob. Imago, our church, is made up of mostly artists and fruit nuts and none of us have any money, so Rick said if I was going to be a writer, I needed to write a bestseller so that the church could have some money.

o o o

I am irresponsible with money if you want to know the truth. I don't have the money to buy big things, thank God, so I buy small things. I like new things too much. I like the way they smell. Today I tried to go to Home Depot to get an extension cord. I need an extension cord to plug in a lamp in the upstairs den. I already bought a timer plug for the lamp, a plug that turns the lamp on in the evening and off after everybody has gone to bed, but now I need an extension cord.

We probably didn't need the timer plug in the first place. I could probably have plugged the lamp into the regular socket and been fine. But when I saw the timer plug at Fred Meyer last week, I stood there looking at it, having come across it by accident, and I realized how very much I needed it. And it was only seven dollars. I need this for seven dollars, I thought to myself, this is very important. I put it into my basket and walked off, wondering what it was that I needed to plug into it. That, of course, is now obvious: the lamp in the upstairs den. I got the timer plug home and programmed it without reading the instructions, then I went to plug the lamp in but the lamp was too far from the outlet. I could not move the lamp closer without ruining the Feng Shui. I have this fruit nut friend who says Feng Shui is very important, that a room should be balanced so that you feel balanced when you are in it. I put the lamp closer to the outlet, and my fruit nut friend was right because I felt very unbalanced. So I would need an extension cord to go with the timer plug.

I only say all this to show you that I have a problem with buying things I really don't need. I saw this documentary about the brain that says habits are formed when the "pleasure center" of the brain lights up as we do a certain behavior. The documentary said that some people's pleasure centers light up when they buy things. I wondered if my pleasure center did that.

Penny thinks I am terrible with the little money I have. I was talking to her the other night, and I mentioned that I was interested in buying a remote control car, and she just sort of sat there and didn't say anything. Penny, are you there? I asked. Yes, she said. What? I asked. Are you serious, Don? Are you going to waste perfectly good money on a remote control car?

"Well . . . uh," I said.

"Well . . . uh . . . Miller, that would be a pretty dumb thing to do when there are children starving in India!" she told me.

I hate it when Penny does this. Honestly, it can be so annoying. She lives it though. She didn't buy clothes for an entire year, her senior year at Reed, because she felt like she was irresponsible with money. She always looked very beautiful anyway, and for her birthday I bought her some mittens at Saturday Market for seven dollars. She wore them like they were from Tiffany's or something. She always talked about them. They weren't that big of a deal, but she hadn't had any new clothes for a year so I think she wore them while she was sleeping or something.

Penny is right about spending money though. Penny is right about everything. Penny said if I were to save about twenty dollars a month and give it to Northwest Medical Teams or Amnesty International, I would literally be saving lives. Literally. But that stupid pleasure center goes off in my brain, and it feels like there is nothing I can do about it. I told Penny about the pleasure center and how I needed the remote control car to make the pleasure center light up, and she just took the phone away from her ear and beat it against her chair.

The thing about the extension cord is I was pretty sure I had one in the basement, in a box with some other cords, but if I looked I might have found it, and then I would not have been able to go to Home Depot. What we needed was a new extension cord, the latest technology, I thought to myself.

I put my boots on very quickly. The good voice, the frugal voice, the Penny voice started inside my head: *Don, please, there are children who could use this money for Christmas presents.* It's August, I said out loud. *What about environmental movements,* Good Voice said, *what about the rain forests that could hold a cure for cancer, a cure for AIDS.* Tree hugger, I said to Good Voice while putting on my motorcycle helmet. *You have a problem,* Good Voice said. You're a pansy, I said back. *You're irresponsible!* Good Voice shouted. Shut your gaping pie hole, I yelled back.

The thing about new things is you feel new when you buy them, you feel as though you are somebody different because you own something different. We are our possessions, you know. There are people who get addicted to buying new stuff. Things. Piles and piles of things. But the new things become old things so quickly. We need new things to replace the old things.

I like things with buttons.

○   ○   ○

A writer I like named Ravi Zacharias says that the heart desires wonder and magic. He says technology is what man uses to supplant the desire for wonder. Ravi Zacharias says that what the heart is really longing to do is worship, to stand in awe of a God we don't understand and can't explain.

I started thinking about what Penny was saying and what Ravi Zacharias says. I was riding my motorcycle down to Home Depot, wondering if Penny and Ravi would make good friends, when I decided I was being stupid, very wasteful and stupid. I knew we had an extension cord in the basement, and I knew I was really going to Home Depot to get some drill bits or a laser level or one of those tap lights, and that I wasn't going to get an extension chord but something else, something I would find when I got there, something that would call to me from its shelf.

At the time I didn't have very much money, and the money I had I needed to learn to use wisely. Money does not belong to me, Rick once told me. Money is God's. He trusts us to dish it out fairly and with a strong degree of charity.

I heard an interview with Bill Gates, and the interviewer asked him if he knew how rich he was, if he could really get his mind around it. He said he couldn't. The only way I can understand it, he said, is that there is nothing I can't buy. If I want something, I can have it. He said that Microsoft saved him because he was really more interested in what he was doing than how much money he had. Lots of rich people are not happy, he said.

Sometimes I am glad I don't have very much money. I think money might own me if I had too much of it. I think I would buy things and not be satisfied with the things I have so I would have to buy more.

Jesus said it is harder for a rich man to enter the kingdom of heaven than for a camel to go through the eye of a needle.

Rick says money should be your tool and that you should control it, it shouldn't control you. This means when I want a new extension cord and I already have one, I should use the one I have and give the rest of the money to people who are having very hard times in their lives. This means I probably didn't need to buy a timer for the lamp. Rick said I should be giving money to Imago-Dei, our church. He said giving 10 percent would be a good place to start. I knew this already. It's called tithing, and somehow it is biblical. The Bible also tells the story of these beautiful people in the very first Christian churches who are giving all their money to the church and the elders are dishing it back out to the community based on need.

o   o   o

One of my good friends, Curt Heidschmidt, gave me a lecture about tithing not very long ago. It was strange to get a lecture about tithing from Curt because Curt is not even a church sort of guy. He goes and all, but he hates it. Usually people who go to church but hate it aren't going around giving lectures about tithing, but Curt gave me a pretty good talking-to.

Curt works at a cabinet shop and cusses all the time and tells dirty jokes. But he tithes, sort of. He used to keep a huge jar on his dresser that was full of money, and when he deposited his paychecks he would pull out 10 percent from the bank. Cold, hard cash. He would take the money home and put it in that jar. The thing must have had a couple thousand dollars in it. I was over one night watching *South Park,* and Curt was griping because the cabinet shop didn't pay him enough so that he could get the motorcycle he wanted.

"Well," I told him, "you must have thousands of dollars in that stinking jar, Curt. Use that." This was before I knew it was his tithing money.

"Can't."

"Why?"

"Can't."

"Why?"

"Isn't mine, Miller." Curt leaned back in his recliner and looked at me over the top of his beer can.

"Isn't yours?" I asked. "Who in the world is storing their savings on your dresser?" I pointed toward his bedroom.

"Well" —he smiled, sort of embarrassed—"it's God's."

"God's?" I shouted.

"Yeah, that's my tithe!" he shouted back.

I was a little shocked, to be honest. Like I said before, he didn't seem like the tithing type. I don't think he even went to church nine out of ten Sundays, and when he did he just grumbled about it.

"Well, why don't you take it down to the church and give it to them?" I asked.

"I haven't been to church in a while, that's why."

"Curt," I told him, "you are the most interesting person I know."

"Thank you, Don. You want a beer?"

"Yes." Curt went over to the fridge and opened a couple of Henry's.

"You tithe, Don?"

I just looked at him. I couldn't believe it. I was about to get a lecture on tithing from a guy who probably subscribed to *Bikes and Babes* magazine.

"Well, Curt, I guess I don't." After I said this, Curt shook his head in disappointment. I started feeling really guilty. "It's a shame, Don." Curt tilted back a bottle as he spoke, punctuating the sentence with a post-swig burp. "You are missing out. I've been tithing since I was a kid. Wouldn't miss a payment to save my life."

"Am I dreaming this?" I asked him.

"Dreaming what, Don?"

"This conversation." When I said this I was pointing back and forth between he and I.

"Don, let me tell you. You should be tithing. That is not your money. That is God's money. You ought to be ashamed of yourself. Stealing from God and all. You write Christian books and everything, and you're not even giving God's money back to Him."

"Well, you don't have to go making me feel all bad about it. You haven't exactly given your money to God either. It's right there on your dresser."

Curt leaned over the big arm of his recliner and with a Jack Nicholson grin on his face said, "Oh, you don't worry about that, big boy. That's God's money, and He's gonna get it. I've never stolen a dime from God, and I'm never gonna start."

I honestly couldn't believe this was happening to me. I go over to Curt's house to watch *South Park,* and I get a guilt trip from a fundamentalist.

Curt went down about two weeks later and turned all his money in to a church secretary. More than three thousand dollars. I started feeling so guilty I couldn't sleep.

I met with Rick after that and confessed I was not giving any money to Imago-Dei. Rick had come over to the house, and we were lying about how much we could bench-press, and then I just blurted it out, "I am not giving any money to the church, Rick. Not a dime."

"Okay," he said. "Interesting way to change the conversation. Why?" he asked. "Why aren't you giving any money to the church?"

"Because I don't have any money. Everything goes to rent and groceries."

"That sounds like a tough situation," he said, very compassionately.

"So am I exempt?" I asked.

"Nope," he said. "We want your cash."

"How much?" I asked.

"How much do you make?"

"I don't know. About a thousand a month, maybe."

"Then we want a hundred. And you should also know how much you make. Part of the benefit of giving a portion of your money is it makes you think about where your money goes. God does not want us to be sloppy with our finances, Don."

"But I need money for rent."

"You also need to trust God."

"I know. I just think it would be easier to trust God if I had extra money to trust Him with."

"That would not be faith, then, would it?"

"No."

"Well, bud, I just want you to know I hate this part of the job, 'cause it sounds like I am asking for your money. I don't care whether or not we have your money. Our needs are met. I want to tell you that you are missing out on so much, Don."

"So much what?"

"The fruit of obedience," he said, looking very pastoral. "When we do what God wants us to do, we are blessed, we are spiritually healthy. God wants us to give a portion of our money to His work on earth. By setting aside money from every check, you are trusting God to provide. He wants you to get over that fear—that fear of trusting Him. It is a scary place, but that is where you have to go as a follower of Christ. There are times when my wife and I don't have enough money to cover bills, but we know the first bill, the first payment we make, is to the church. That is most important. If the other bills get neglected, then we need to watch how we are spending money. And there are times when we have found ourselves in that situation. But it works out. We are getting good at trusting God, and we are getting good at managing money."

The next week I emptied my checking account, which had about eight dollars in it, and I gave it to the church. Another check came a few days later, and I gave 10 percent of that to the church, then I got another writing gig with a magazine in Atlanta, and as I deposited that check into my account I wrote a check to the church. One after another, I started getting called to speak at retreats and conferences that usually pay pretty well, and each time I would write a check to the church. Since then, since that conversation with Rick, I have given at least 10 percent of every dollar I make, just like Curt. And I have never not had rent. For more than a year my checking account had hovered or dipped just over or just under zero, and suddenly I had money to spare. I decided I would open a savings account in case some day I would get married and have a family, and with each bit of money that came in I would give 10 percent to the church and 10 percent to the savings account. I was actually budgeting money. I had never done that before.

But that is not the best part. The best part is what tithing has done for my relationship with God. Before, I felt like I was always going to God with my fingers crossed, the way a child feels around his father when he knows he has told terrible lies. God knew where I was, He didn't love me any different when I was holding out on Him, it's just that I didn't feel clean around Him, and you know how that can affect things.

I also learned that I needed to give to the poor. My church gives money to the poor, but it was also important for me to give directly to the poor. I would go downtown sometimes and buy a homeless person lunch. I hated it at first because I always stumbled across the guys with terrible table manners, but after a while I began to like their drunken ramblings. Even though they weren't making any sense, they thought they were, and that has to count for something.

○   ○   ○

We don't need as much money as we have. Hardly any of us need as much money as we have. It's true what they say about the best things in life being free.

For a little while, a long time ago, I was a minimalist. I wasn't a minimalist on purpose, it's just that my friend Paul and I had been traveling around the country living in a van, like I mentioned earlier. We eventually ran out of money, so we sold the van and lived in the woods. We lived in the Cascade Mountains for a month. We walked through the woods into a resort every day where I scrubbed toilets in condos and Paul worked as a lifeguard. I ate the food people would leave in the refrigerator after they had checked out. Mostly perishables. Ice cream. Fruit. Cheese.

I only tell you this because when we were living in the woods, we didn't worry about anything, especially about money. After about a week I stopped wondering if food was going to show. I learned that people throw tons of food away, and there will always be plenty. I didn't think about rent because I didn't pay rent; the forest is free, it turns out, great property all over. There I was, living in one of the most beautiful territories in all of America, eating free food and sleeping under the stars. It did not take long for that nagging feeling of fear, the false feeling of security that money gives us, to subside.

I remember a particular midnight, three weeks into our stay, walking into a meadow surrounded by thick aspens and above me all that glorious heaven glowing, and I felt like I was a part of it, what with the trees clapping hands and me feeling like I was floating there beneath the endlessness. I looked up so long I felt like I was in space. Light. No money and no anxiety.

It is possible to feel that way again. It is possible not to let possessions own me, to rest happily in the security that God, not money, can give. I have been feeling that a little lately. Rick asked me how I was doing with the money thing, with the tithe thing, and I told him I was on the up-and-up. He asked me how I was feeling about all of that, and I told him I was feeling good, free, light. He told me not to get a big head about it.

17

Worship

The Mystical Wonder

I READ A BOOK A LONG TIME AGO ABOUT MOTHER Teresa. Somebody in the book asked her how she summoned the strength to love so many people. She said she loved people because they are Jesus, each one of them is Jesus, and this is true because it says so in the Bible. And it is also true that this idea contradicts the facts of reality: Everybody can't be Jesus. There are many ideas within Christian spirituality that contradict the facts of reality as I understand them. A statement like this offends some Christians because they believe if aspects of their faith do not obey the facts of reality, they are not true. But I think there are all sorts of things our hearts believe that don't make any sense to our heads. Love, for instance; we believe in love. Beauty. Jesus as God.

It comforts me to think that if we are created beings, the thing that created us would have to be greater than us, so much greater, in fact, that we would not be able to understand it. It would have to be greater than the facts of our reality, and so it would seem to us, looking out from within our reality, that it would contradict reason. But reason itself would suggest it would have to be greater than reality, or it would not be reasonable.

When we worship God we worship a Being our life experience does not give us the tools with which to understand. If we could, God would not inspire awe. Eternity, for example, is not something the human mind can understand. We may be able to wrap our heads around living forever (and we can do this only because none of us has experienced death), but can we understand what it means to have never been born? I only say this to illustrate that we, as Christians, believe things we cannot explain. And so does everybody else.

I have a friend who is a seminary student who criticizes certain Christian writers for embracing what he calls "mysticism." I asked him if his statement meant that he was not a mystic. Of course not, he told me. I asked him if he believed in the Trinity. He said he did. I asked him if he believed that the Trinity represented three separate persons who are also one. He said he did. I asked him if that would be considered a mystical idea. He just stood there thinking.

You cannot be a Christian without being a mystic.

I was talking to a homeless man at a laundry mat recently, and he said that when we reduce Christian spirituality to math we defile the Holy. I thought that was very beautiful and comforting because I have never been good at math. Many of our attempts to understand Christian faith have only cheapened it. I can no more understand the totality of God than the pancake I made for breakfast understands the complexity of me. The little we do understand, that grain of sand our minds are capable of grasping, those ideas such as God is good, God feels, God loves, God knows all, are enough to keep our hearts dwelling on His majesty and otherness forever.

o   o   o

Here is one of the coolest things I ever did: This past summer I made a point to catch sunsets. I would ride my motorcycle up

Mount Tabor and sit on the steps of the reservoir to watch the sun put fire in the clouds that are always hanging over Portland. I never really wanted to make the trip; I would want to watch television or make a sandwich, but I made myself go. And once I got up there I always loved it. It always meant something to me to see beauty right there over my city.

My first sunset this year was the most spectacular. Forest fires in Washington State blew a light, nearly unnoticeable haze through Portland, and the clouds were just low enough to catch the full reflection of red and yellow. I thought to myself, *This is something that happens all the time.* From the ridge on Tabor where I planted myself, I could see the entire skyline, the home of more than a million people. On most nights there were no more than two or three people there with me. All that beauty happens right above the heads of more than a million people who never notice it.

Here is what I've started thinking: All the wonder of God happens right above our arithmetic and formula. The more I climb outside my pat answers, the more invigorating the view, the more my heart enters into worship.

o   o   o

I love how the Gospels start, with John the Baptist eating bugs and baptizing people. The religious people started getting baptized because it had become popular, and John yells at them and calls them snakes. He says the water won't do anything for them, it will only get their snakeskins wet. But if they meant it, if they had faith that Jesus was coming and was real, then Jesus would ignite the kingdom life within them. I love that because for so long religion was my false gospel. But there was no magic in it, no wonder, no awe, no kingdom life burning in my chest. And when I get tempted by that same stupid Christian religion, I go back to the beginning of the Gospels and am comforted that there is something more than the emptiness of ritual. God will ignite the kingdom life within me, the Bible says. That's mysticism. It isn't a formula that I am figuring out. It is something God does.

One night I watched the sunset till the stars faded in and, while looking up, my mind, or my heart, I do not know which, realized how endless it all was. I laid myself down on some grass and reached my hand directly out toward where? I don't know. There is no up and down. There has never been an up and down. Things like up and down were invented so as not to scare children, so as to reduce mystery to math. The truth is we do not know there is an end to material existence. It may go on forever, which is something the mind cannot understand.

My friend Jason and I went on a trip to Joshua Tree and Death Valley, and he had a map folded across his lap nearly the entire trip. Even when I was driving, he had the map out, following along with his finger the trajectory of the car, noting how close we were to certain towns, certain lakes. Jason liked to know where we were on the map (and so did I, as a matter of fact). But I was afraid to tell Jason about the universe, how scientists haven't found the edge of it, of how nobody knows exactly where we are on the map.

I think we have two choices in the face of such big beauty: terror or awe. And this is precisely why we attempt to chart God, because we want to be able to predict Him, to dissect Him, to carry Him around in our dog and pony show. We are too proud to feel awe and too fearful to feel terror. We reduce Him to math so we don't have to fear Him, and yet the Bible tells us fear is the appropriate response, that it is the beginning of wisdom. Does this mean God is going to hurt us? No. But I stood on the edge of the Grand Canyon once, behind a railing, and though I was never going to fall off the edge, I feared the thought of it. It is that big of a place, that wonderful of a landscape.

○   ○   ○

I like that scene in the movie *Dead Poets Society* in which Mr. Keating, an English instructor at an elite preparatory school, asks his students to rip out the "Introduction to Poetry" essay from their literature textbooks. The essayist had instructed students in a method of grading poems on a sliding scale, complete with the use of a grid, thus reducing art for the heart into arithmetic for the head. The students looked around at each other in confusion as their teacher dismissed the essay as rubbish and ordered them to rip these pages from their books. And at their teacher's loud prodding, the students began to rip. Dr. Keating paced the aisle with a trash can and reminded the students that poetry is not algebra, not songs on *American Bandstand* that can be rated on a scale from one to ten, but rather they are pieces of art that plunge the depths of the heart to stir vigor in men and woo women.

Too much of our time is spent trying to chart God on a grid, and too little is spent allowing our hearts to feel awe. By reducing Christian spirituality to formula, we deprive our hearts of wonder.

When I think about the complexity of the Trinity, the three-in-one God, my mind cannot understand, but my heart feels wonder in abundant satisfaction. It is as though my heart, in the midst of its euphoria, is saying to my mind, *There are things you cannot understand, and you must learn to live with this. Not only must you learn to live with this, you must learn to enjoy this.*

I want to tell you something about me that you may see as weakness. I need wonder. I know that death is coming. I smell it in the wind, read it in the paper, watch it on television, and see it on the faces of the old. I need wonder to explain what is going to happen to me, what is going to happen to us when this thing is done, when our shift is over and our kids' kids are still on the earth listening to their crazy rap music. I need something mysterious to happen after I die. I need to be somewhere else after I die, somewhere with God, somewhere that wouldn't make any sense if it were explained to me right now.

At the end of the day, when I am lying in bed and I know the chances of any of our theology being exactly right are a million to one, I need to know that God has things figured out, that if my math is wrong we are still going to be okay. And wonder is that feeling we get when we let go of our silly answers, our mapped out rules that we want God to follow. I don't think there is any better worship than wonder.

(18)

Love

How to Really Love Other People

WHEN MY FRIEND PAUL AND I LIVED IN THE woods, we lived with hippies. Well, sort of hippies. They certainly smoked a lot of pot. They drank a lot of beer. And man did they love each other, sometimes too much, perhaps, too physically, you know, but nonetheless they loved; they accepted and cherished everybody, even the ones who judged them because they were hippies. It was odd living with the hippies at first, but I enjoyed it after a while.

They were not the traveling hippies, the "live off the land and other people" hippies. They were formally educated, most of them from New York studying at NYU, getting their master's in literature, headed off to law school, that sort of thing. They knew all about Rostandt, all about Hopkins and Poe and Sylvia Plath. They knew the Americans and the Brits and the fashionable African writers, the Cubans and South Americans. They were books themselves, all of them were books, and what was so wonderful is that to them, I was a book too. We would sit around and talk about literature and each other, and I couldn't tell the difference between the books they were talking about and their lives, they were just that cool. I liked them very much because they were interested in me. When I was with the hippies I did not feel judged, I felt loved. To them I was an endless well of stories and perspectives and grand literary views. It felt so wonderful to be in their presence, like I was special.

I have never experienced a group of people who loved each other more than my hippies in the woods. All of them are tucked so neatly into my memory now, and I recall our evenings at camp or in the meadow or in the caves in my mind like a favorite film. I pull them out when I need to be reminded about goodness, about purity and kindness.

The resort we were working at was Black Butte Ranch in central Oregon, and we were living about a mile off a ridge, beyond the cattle fence, down in a gully where stood stately pines and remarkable aspen. There were also a family of deer and a porcupine. The boys from New York worked at Honkers Café, named for the ducks, and Paul and I would merely have to sit ourselves on the deck off the lake and within minutes we would have a burger or a shake or a slice of pie, always delivered with a smile, always for free. They were stealing from the rich to feed the poor. We were eating food from the wealthy table of the white man. This is how I thought about it, even though I was white.

After Honker's closed we would fill the café and play the juke box, the guys always choosing Springsteen and talking about life in New York, about life in the city. But more than they talked, they listened.

So much of what I know about getting along with people I learned from the hippies. They were magical in community. People were drawn to them. They asked me what I loved, what I hated, how I felt about this and that, what sort of music made me angry, what sort of music made me sad. They asked me what I daydreamed about, what I wrote about, where my favorite places in the world were. They asked me about high school and college and my travels around America. They loved me like a good novel, like an art film, and this is how I felt when I was with them, like a person John Irving would write. I did not feel fat or stupid or sloppily dressed. I did not feel like I did not know the Bible well enough, and I was never conscious what my hands were doing or whether or not I sounded immature when I talked. I had always been so conscious of those things, but living with the hippies I forgot about myself. And when I lost this self-consciousness I gained so much more. I gained an interest in people outside my own skin. They were greater than movies to me, greater than television. The spirit of the hippies was contagious. I couldn't hear enough about Eddie's ballerina girlfriend or Owen's epic poems. I would ask them to repeat stories because, to me, they were like great scenes in favorite movies. I cannot tell you how quickly these people, these pot-smoking hippies, disarmed me.

Because I grew up in the safe cocoon of big-Christianity, I came to believe that anything outside the church was filled with darkness and unlove. I remember, one Sunday evening, sitting in the pew as a child listening to the pastor read from articles in the newspaper. He took an entire hour to flip through the paper reading about all the gory murders and rapes and burglaries, and after each article he would sigh and say, *Friends, it is a bad, bad world out there. And things are only getting worse.* Never in my wildest dreams would I have imagined there were, outside the church, people so purely lovely as the ones I met in the woods. And yet my hippie friends were not at all close to believing that Christ was the Son of God.

This did not confuse me so much as it surprised me. Until this point, the majority of my friends had been Christians. In fact nearly all of them had been Christians. I was amazed to find, outside the church, genuine affection being shared, affection that seemed, well, authentic in comparison to the sort of love I had known within the church. I was even more amazed when I realized I preferred, in fact, the company of the hippies to the company of Christians. It isn't that I didn't love my Christian friends or that they didn't love me, it was just that there was something different about my hippie friends; something, I don't know, more real, more true. I realize that is a provocative statement, but I only felt I could be myself around them, and I could not be myself with my Christian friends. My Christian communities had always had little unwritten social ethics like don't cuss and don't support Democrats and don't ask tough questions about the Bible.

I stayed in the woods only a month. I wanted to stay longer, but I had secured a job in Colorado at a Christian camp and needed to honor that agreement. Though I had spent only a month with the hippies, it seemed a lifetime. I had learned more about people, about community and happiness and contentment by living in the woods than I had in a lifetime of studying these ideas philosophically. I had discovered life outside the church, and I liked it. As I said, I preferred it. I said my sad good-byes and boarded a bus bound for Colorado.

o   o   o

Before getting off the Greyhound bus, I threw away my pack of cigarettes. I knew I would not be able to smoke while working at camp. The guy who picked me up from the bus station could smell the smoke on my clothes so he sat quietly and asked few questions. Though Paul and I had been in the woods for only a month, we had been traveling around America for several months, and so the first thing I noticed when I got to camp was that these were clean people; they ironed their clothes and that sort of thing. They had clean-shaven faces and spoke through smiles.

I liked them, they all looked so new to me, so much like they belonged in storefront windows, like fine china dolls or models for Banana Republic. There was a buzz about me almost immediately. I didn't want there to be, but I had been traveling for so long I'd forgotten some basic things like sleeping indoors and eating with utensils. Some of the bolder staff members approached me to try to talk. I think they thought I was sort of stupid because they spoke very slowly and made wide motions with their hands as they spoke. "I'm Jane. My name, Jane, what your name?"

The camp director, a very conservative man, sent word to me through a servant that I was to shave and wear appropriate clothes. It is true I had gotten a little hairy in the woods. They had rules, these people, they had expectations, and if you did not comply you were socially shunned. Well, not really shunned, just smiled at, smiled at a great deal, smiled at and watched and giggled over when passed in the hall. I confess I enjoyed being different. I got more attention by being the hippie guy than I had when I was normal. I felt better in a lot of ways, more superior, because I was no longer sheltered. I had been in the world, and the world had approved of me.

They were cute, these little Christian people. I liked them. They reminded me of my roots, where I had come from all those days ago, before my month in the woods with the pot smokers and the hippies and the free love for everybody. When the director's assistant told me to shave she told me sheepishly. She knew it was a silly request. Hey, listen, I told her, I will do exactly what the man tells me to do, you know, because I respect the man, I don't want a fight. She smiled back at me, seeing the genius of my emotional intelligence.

"Do you need a razor or something?" She looked at me, sort of smirking.

"You know," I replied, leaning against the wall in the hallway,

"I think I have one somewhere; I have a backpack or something somewhere."

"You don't know where your stuff is?" she asked, obviously coming from a primitive, materialistic, territorial paradigm.

"Oh, you know, it is probably in my room, or maybe around, you know, who knows?"

"Well maybe you should put it somewhere where you won't lose it."

"Well, you know, if I lost it, what would I have lost, right?" I asked her.

"You would have lost your backpack," she answered matter-of-factly. She had sort of a bothered, questioning look on her face.

"Right. Right, but you know, what would any of us lose by losing our possessions. Maybe we would gain something, like relationships, like the beauty of good friends, intimacy, you know what I mean, man? Like we wouldn't be losing anything if we lost our stuff, we'd be gaining everything."

"Yeah," she said. "That's fascinating. Well, just shave, okay. If you need a razor I will get you one." She was getting very flustered or something, really wanting to pull out of the conversation. I figured she hadn't met anybody fascinating like me before.

"Yeah," I told her. "Yeah, if I need anything I will come looking for you. That's sweet of you, real sweet."

"Honestly, it's my job," she told me.

"Cool. That's chill," I said.

"What?"

"That's chill. You know, on ice."

"Right." She said this very slowly. She stood there silently, just looking at me like I was a big, mysterious puzzle.

"So tell me," I said, breaking the silence, "what do your people call you?"

"My people?"

"Yeah, like your friends, your close ones."

"Are you asking my name?"

"Right on. Your name. What's your name?"

"Janet."

"Janet. Right. Janet. Planet Janet from the Jupiter scene."

Long pause.

"Right," she said slowly.

"So are you in school, Janet? Like, are you in college or just the school of life?"

"I was homeschooled. I'm going to Bob Jones next year."

"Bob who?"

"Jones. It's a college."

"Cool. That's chill."

"Listen, Dan," she started.

"Don," I corrected her. "My name is Don, actually."

"Right," she said slowly. "Is that what your people call you?"

"Yeah." I think she might have been making fun of me or flirting or something.

"You should probably shave," she continued. "And I wasn't going to tell you, but maybe you should take a shower." She was definitely flirting.

"No prob, Janet, you know, thanks for mentioning it. I've been living in the woods, you know, out in the open and all. Don't need a shower out there, right?"

"Not out there, no. But since you will be with us now, you know, maybe you should try it out."

"Right on. Cool to know the rules, you know."

"Well, Don, it was certainly interesting meeting you. I am sure I will see you again. Maybe won't recognize you though." She motioned toward my beard and smiled.

I didn't know what she meant at first, but then I got it. She meant she wouldn't recognize me after I shaved. "Oh, yeah, cool," I told her. "Maybe not, huh? But don't worry, I will remind you who I am."

"Right," she said slowly, and then walked away shaking her head.

○   ○   ○

While at camp we were encouraged to attend church. Buses went on Sundays to a couple of different churches. Both of them were a little stiff.

I felt like both churches came to the table with a them and us mentality, them being the liberal non-Christians in the world, and us being Christians. I felt, once again, that there was this underlying hostility for homosexuals and Democrats and, well, hippie types. I cannot tell you how much I did not want liberal or gay people to be my enemies. I liked them. I cared about them, and they cared about me. I learned that in the woods. I had never felt so alive as I did in the company of my liberal friends. It isn't that the Christians I had been with had bad community; they didn't, I just liked the community of the hippies because it was more forgiving, more, I don't know, healthy.

The real issue in the Christian community was that it was conditional. You were loved, but if you had questions, questions about whether the Bible was true or whether America was a good country or whether last week's sermon was good, you were not so loved. You were loved in word, but there was, without question, a social commodity that was being withheld from you until you shaped up. By toeing the party line you earned social dollars; by being yourself you did not. If you wanted to be valued, you became a clone. These are broad generalizations, and they are unfair, but this is what I was thinking at the time. Bear with me, and I will tell you what I learned.

I began to attend a Unitarian church. All-Souls Unitarian Church in Colorado Springs was wonderful. The people were wonderful. Like my friends in the woods, they freely and openly accepted everybody the church didn't seem to accept. I don't suppose they accepted fundamentalists, but neither did I at the time. I was comfortable there. Everybody was comfortable there. I did not like their flaky theology though. I did not like the way they changed words in the hymns, and I did not like the fact they ignored the Bible, but I loved them, and they really liked me. I loved the smiley faces, the hugs, the vulnerable feel to the place, the wonderful old gray-haired professors, former alcoholics and drug addicts, the intellectual feminists who greeted me with the kindest, most authentic faces that I understood as invitations to tell my story.

I began to understand that my pastors and leaders were wrong, that the liberals were not evil, they were liberal for the same reason Christians were Christians, because they believed their philosophies were right, good, and beneficial for the world. I had been raised to believe there were monsters under the bed, but I had peeked, in a moment of bravery, and found a wonderful world, a good world, better, in fact, than the one I had known.

The problem with Christian community was that we had ethics, we had rules and laws and principles to judge each other against. There was love in Christian community, but it was conditional love. Sure, we called it unconditional, but it wasn't. There were bad people in the world and good people in the world. We were raised to believe this. If people were bad, we treated them as though they were either evil or charity: If they were bad and rich, they were evil. If they were bad and poor, they were charity. Christianity was always right; we were always looking down on everybody else. And I hated this. I hated it with a passion. Everything in my soul told me it was wrong. It felt, to me, as wrong as sin. I wanted to love everybody. I wanted everything to be cool. I realize this sounds like tolerance, and to many in the church the word *tolerance* is profanity, but that is precisely what I wanted. I wanted tolerance. I wanted everybody to leave everybody else alone, regardless of their religious beliefs, regardless of their political affiliation. I wanted people to like each other. Hatred seemed, to me, the product of ignorance. I was tired of biblical ethic being used as a tool with which to judge people rather than heal them. I was tired of Christian leaders using biblical principles to protect their power, to draw a line in the sand separating the good army from the bad one. The truth is I had met the enemy in the woods and discovered they were not the enemy. I wondered whether any human being could be an enemy of God.

On the other hand, however, I felt by loving liberal people, I mean by really endorsing their existence, I was betraying the truth of God because I was encouraging them in their lives apart from God. I felt like there was this war going on between us, the Christians, and them, the homosexuals and environmentalists and feminists. By going to a Unitarian church and truly loving those people, I was helping them, I was giving joy to their life and that didn't feel right. It was a terrible place to be.

This was, at the time, my primary problem with Christian faith. With all its talk about pure love, in the end it shook down to conditional love. Again, this is a provocative statement, but I want to walk you through the emotional process I went through.

How could I merge the culture of the woods and the Unitarian church with Christian culture and yet not abandon the truth of Scripture? How could I love my neighbor without endorsing what, I truly believed, was unhealthy spirituality?

My answer did not come for many years, and as for that summer, I became very confused. I gave in to keep the peace. I stopped going to the Unitarian church, I shaved, I cut the hippy act and made friends, good friends, friends whom I loved and who loved me. From time to time I would overhear comments by my friends, destructive comments about the political left or about homosexuals or Democrats, and I never knew what to do with those comments. They felt right in my head but not in my heart. I went along, and, looking back, I think we all went along. Even the people who were making the comments were going along. What else was there to do? Truth is truth.

○　○　○

It is always the simple things that change our lives. And these things never happen when you are looking for them to happen. Life will reveal answers at the pace life wishes to do so. You feel like running, but life is on a stroll. This is how God does things.

My realization came while attending an alumni social for Westmont College. I had never attended Westmont, but my friend Michelle did, and she invited me. Greg Spencer, a communications professor, was to speak, and Michelle thought I might enjoy the lecture. I did. More than I can say. The lecture was about the power of metaphor. Spencer opened by asking us what metaphors we think of when we consider the topic of cancer. We gave him our answers, all pretty much the same, we *battle* cancer, we *fight* cancer, we are rebuilding our white blood cells, things like that. Spencer pointed out that the overwhelming majority of metaphors we listed were war metaphors. They dealt with battle. He then proceeded to talk about cancer patients and how, because of war metaphor, many people who suffer with cancer feel more burdened than, in fact, they should. Most of them are frightened beyond their need to be frightened, and this affects their health. Some, feeling that they have been thrust into a deadly war, simply give up. If there were another metaphor, a metaphor more accurate, perhaps cancer would not prove so deadly.

Science has shown that the way people think about cancer affects their ability to deal with the disease, thus affecting their overall health. Professor Spencer said that if he were to sit down with his family and tell them he had cancer they would be shocked, concerned, perhaps even in tears, and yet cancer is nothing near the most deadly of diseases. Because of war metaphor, the professor said, we are more likely to fear cancer when, actually, most people survive the disease.

Mr. Spencer then asked us about another area in which he felt metaphors cause trouble. He asked us to consider relationships. What metaphors do we use when we think of relationships? We *value* people, I shouted out. Yes, he said, and wrote it on his little white board. We *invest* in people, another person added. And soon enough we had listed an entire white board of economic metaphor. Relationships could be *bankrupt*, we said. People are *priceless*, we said. All economic metaphor. I was taken aback.

And that's when it hit me like so much epiphany getting dislodged from my arteries. The problem with Christian culture is we think of love as a commodity. We use it like money. Professor Spencer was right, and not only was he right, I felt as though he had cured me, as though he had let me out of my cage. I could see it very clearly. If somebody is doing something for us, offering us something, be it gifts, time, popularity, or what have you, we feel they have value, we feel they are worth something to us, and, perhaps, we feel they are priceless. I could see it so clearly, and I could feel it in the pages of my life. This was the thing that had smelled so rotten all these years. I used love like money. The church used love like money. With love, we withheld affirmation from the people who did not agree with us, but we lavishly financed the ones who did.

The next few days unfolded in a thick line of melancholy thought and introspection. I used love like money, but love doesn't work like money. It is not a commodity. When we barter with it, we all lose. When the church does not love its enemies, it fuels their rage. It makes them hate us more.

Here's how it worked out on a personal level:

There was this guy in my life at the time, a guy I went to church with whom I honestly didn't like. I thought he was sarcastic and lazy and manipulative, and he ate with his mouth open so that food almost fell from his chin when he talked. He began and ended every sentence with the word *dude*.

"Dude, did you see Springer yesterday?" he would say. "They had this fat lady on there who was doing it with a midget. It was crazy, dude. I want to get me a midget, dude."

That's the sort of thing he would talk about. It was very interesting to him. I don't enjoy not liking people, but sometimes these things feel as though you are not in control of them. I never chose not to like the guy. It felt more like the dislike of him chose me. Regardless, I had to spend a good amount of time with him as we were working on a temporary project together. He began to get under my skin. I wanted him to change. I wanted him to read a book, memorize a poem, or explore morality, at least as an intellectual concept. I didn't know how to communicate to him that he needed to change, so I displayed it on my face. I rolled my eyes. I gave him dirty looks. I would mouth the word *loser* when he wasn't looking. I thought somehow he would sense my disapproval and change his life in order to gain my favor. In short, I withheld love.

After Greg Spencer's lecture, I knew what I was doing was wrong. It was selfish, and what's more, it would never work. By withholding love from my friend, he became defensive, he didn't like me, he thought I was judgmental, snobbish, proud, and mean. Rather than being drawn to me, wanting to change, he was repulsed. I was guilty of using love like money, withholding it to get somebody to be who I wanted them to be. I was making a mess of everything. And I was disobeying God. I became convicted about these things, so much so that I had some trouble getting sleep. It was clear that I was to love everybody, be delighted at everybody's existence, and I had fallen miles short of God's aim. The power of Christian spirituality has always rested in repentance, so that's what I did. I repented. I told God I was sorry. I replaced economic metaphor, in my mind, with something different, a free gift metaphor or a magnet metaphor. That is, instead of withholding love to change somebody, I poured it on, lavishly. I hoped that love would work like a magnet, pulling people from the mire and toward healing. I knew this was the way God loved me. God had never withheld love to teach me a lesson.

Here is something very simple about relationships that Spencer helped me discover: Nobody will listen to you unless they sense that you like them.

If a person senses that you do not like them, that you do not approve of their existence, then your religion and your political ideas will all seem wrong to them. If they sense that you like them, then they are open to what you have to say.

After I repented, things were different, but the difference wasn't with my friend, the difference was with me. I was happy. Before, I had all this negative tension flipping around in my gut, all this judgmentalism and pride and loathing of other people. I hated it, and now I was set free. I was free to love. I didn't have to discipline anybody, I didn't have to judge anybody, I could treat everybody as though they were my best friend, as though they were rock stars or famous poets, as though they were amazing, and to me they became amazing, especially my new friend. I loved him. After I decided to let go of judging him, I discovered he was very funny. I mean, really hilarious. I kept telling him how funny he was. And he was smart. Quite brilliant, really. I couldn't believe that I had never seen it before. I felt as though I had lost an enemy and gained a brother. And then he began to change. It didn't matter to me whether he did or not, but he did. He began to get a little more serious about God. He gave up television for a period of time as a sort of fast. He started praying and got regular about going to church. He was a great human being getting even better. I could feel God's love for him. I loved the fact that it wasn't my responsibility to change somebody, that it was God's, that my part was just to communicate love and approval.

When I am talking to somebody there are always two conversations going on. The first is on the surface; it is about politics or music or whatever it is our mouths are saying. The other is beneath the surface, on the level of the heart, and my heart is either communicating that I like the person I am talking to or I don't. God wants both conversations to be true. That is, we are supposed to speak truth in love. If both conversations are not true, God is not involved in the exchange, we are on our own, and on our own, we will lead people astray. The Bible says that if you talk to somebody with your mouth, and your heart does not love them, that you are like a person standing there smashing two cymbals together. You are only annoying everybody around you. I think that is very beautiful and true.

Now, since Greg Spencer told me about truth, when I go to meet somebody, I pray that God will help me feel His love for them. I ask God to make it so both conversations, the one from the mouth and the one from the heart, are true.

Love

How to Really Love Yourself

I WISH ANI DIFRANCO WASN'T A LESBIAN. I AM listening to her right now, and I think I would marry her if she would have me. I would hang out in the front row at all her concerts and sing along and pump my fist and get angry at all the right times. Then, later, on the bus, she would lay her head on a pillow in my lap, and I would get my fingers tangled in her dreadlocks while we watched Charlie Rose on the television.

Some friends and I were walking to our cars one night outside the Roseland after an Emmy Lou Harris concert, and I could see into her bus and Charlie Rose was on the television. I thought to myself, *I like that show,* and part of me wanted to knock on the window and ask if I could come in. I would not have bothered her or even asked for an autograph. I would have just watched television. He was interviewing Bishop Tutu, I think. By the time I got home the interview was over. If Ani Defranco and I got married, I would write books on the bus rides between cities and in the evening, after the concerts, we would watch Charlie Rose, and three or four times each night we would whisper, *Good question, Charlie, good question.* But none of this will happen because Ani Difranco is not attracted to men, I don't think. Otherwise we would be on.

○　○　○

The thing about Reed College you may not know is that it is a beautiful place. I mean the people are beautiful, and I love them. My housemate, Grant, and I were on campus the other day helping kids move into their dorms, and we met this kid Nathan, who needed us to move a couch up to his room. Grant and I were sort of surprised when Nathan started talking to us because, no kidding, he sounded just like Elmer Fudd. He was short and stocky, and nobody but Elmer Fudd himself sounds more like Elmer Fudd than Nathan. Grant almost started laughing, but we tried very hard to listen to the person inside the voice, and so on the way to the storage shed Nathan opened up and told us that as a summer job he worked at Los Alamos, researching nuclear weapons. Nathan does not know his left from his right, which I thought was a peculiar characteristic, given he is one of the smartest people in the world or something. We would come to an intersection and he would point and say, in a perfect Elmer Fudd dialect (I can't do accents at all), "Go dat way, Don. Dat ith de way to de thorage thed."

I was speaking at a pastors conference in San Francisco, and I was telling them about my friends from Reed and what it looks like to talk about Jesus in that place. Somebody asked me what it was like to deal with all the immorality at Reed, and that question really struck me because I have never thought of Reed as an immoral place, and I suppose I never thought of it as an immoral place because somebody like Nathan can go there and talk like Elmer Fudd, and nobody will ever make fun of him. And if Nathan were to go to my church, which I love and would give my life for, he would unfortunately be made fun of by somebody somewhere, behind his back and all, but it would happen, and that is such a tragic crime. Nobody would bother to find out that he is a genius. Nobody would know that he is completely comfortable talking the way he talks and not knowing his left from his right because he has spent four years in a place where what you are on the surface does not define you, it does not label you. And that is what I love about Reed College because even though there are so many students having sex and tripping on drugs and whatever, there is also this foundational understanding that other people exist and they are important, and to me Reed is like heaven in that sense. I wish everybody could spend four years in a place like that, being taught the truth, that they matter regardless of their faults, regardless of their insecurities.

o   o   o

Television drives me crazy sometimes because everybody is so good-looking, and yet you walk through the aisles of the grocery stores, and nobody looks like that. Somebody told me that in London people don't judge you as much by the way you look, and I think it is true because late night on PBS they play shows out of England and the actors aren't good-looking, and I sit there wondering if anybody else is watching and asking the same question: Why aren't the actors in London good looking? And I already know the answer to that question, it is that America is one of the most immoral countries in the world and that our media has reduced humans to slabs of meat. And there will always be this tension while I live in this country because none of this will ever change. Ani Difranco, in her song "32 Flavors," says that she is *a poster girl with no poster, she is 32 flavors and then some, and she is beyond our peripheral vision, so we might want to turn our heads, because some day we're gonna get hungry and eat all of the words we just said.* And just about everybody I know loves those lines because they speak of heaven and of hope and the idea that some day a King will come and dictate, through some mystical act of love, an existence in which everybody has to eat their own words because we won't be allowed to judge each other on the surface of things anymore. And this fills me with hope.

Jean-Paul Sarte said hell is other people. But that Indian speaker I really like named Ravi Zacharias says that heaven can be other people, too, and that we have the power to bring a little of heaven into the lives of others every day. I know this is true because I have felt it when Penny or Tony tells me I mean something to them and they love me. I pray often that God would give me the strength and dignity to receive their love.

My friend Julie from Seattle says the key to everything rests in the ability to receive love, and what she says is right because my personal experience tells me so. I used to not be able to receive love at all, and to this day I have some problems, but it isn't like it used to be. My eye would find things on television and in the media and somehow I would compare myself to them without really knowing I was doing it, and this really screwed me up because I never for a second felt I was worthy of anybody's compliments.

o   o   o

I was dating this girl for a while, this cute writer from the South, and she was great, really the perfect girl, and we shared tastes on everything from music to movies, all the important stuff, and yet I could not really thrive in the relationship because I could never believe her deeply when she expressed affection. Our love was never a two-way conversation. I didn't realize I was doing it, but

I used to kick myself around quite a bit in my head, calling myself a loser and that sort of thing. There was nothing this girl could do to get through to me. She would explain her feelings, and I should have been happy with that, but I always needed more and then I resented the fact that I needed more because, well, it is such a needy thing to need more, and so I lived inside this conflict. I would sit on the porch at Graceland and watch cars go around the circle while all this stuff went around in my heart. There was no peace at all. I couldn't eat. I couldn't sleep.

Andrew the Protester, the one who looks like Fidel Castro, was living in the house back then, and he is such an amazing listener that I would talk to him and he would nod his head and say, "Don, man, I didn't know you were feeling any of this." But I was. And it got worse. I would mope around the house all day, and I couldn't get any writing done. It had been the same in all my relationships. There was always, within me, this demand for affection, this needy, clingy monkey on my back. I wouldn't be satisfied unless the girl wanted to get married right away, unless she was panicky about it, and even then I would imagine a non-existent scenario in which she finds another man or breaks up with me because of the way I look. I would find myself getting depressed about conversations that never even took place.

Finally, Andrew said I should meet with Diane, who is this beautiful married woman who goes to our church and mothers us and speaks love into our lives because most of us are basket cases. Diane was studying at a local seminary to be a counselor, and Andrew recommended that I ask her to take a shot at all my troubles. I didn't want to do it at first because Diane's husband is an elder, and I had spoken at church a few times, so everybody thought I was normal. Certainly if I talked to Diane she would go home and tell her husband I was nuts and then it would get around the church, and when everybody thinks you are nuts you finally just give in to their pressure and actually go nuts. But I was desperate. So I called Diane.

She was beautiful and soft and kind with a tender voice, and she showed up at the house, and I put some coffee on. We went into my office, and I closed the door, in case one of my room-mates walked by and saw me talking to Diane and discovered I was nuts. I sat in a chair, and Diane sat on the couch, and I wrung my hands a bit before starting in:

"Well, you see, Diane, I am in this relationship with this girl, and she is great, she really is. It's just that it is very hard for me, you know."

"You mean it is hard for you to have feelings for her?"

"I'm not gay."

Diane laughed. "I didn't mean it that way, Don."

"I do have feelings for her," I said, with sincerity. "They are almost too strong, you know. I have trouble sleeping and eating and thinking about anything else. It is hard for me to be in a rela-tionship, it always has been. And that makes me want to bail. I would just rather not be in the relationship at all than go through this torture. But I promised myself I wouldn't run from it this time. But I feel like the meaning of life is riding on whether or not she likes me, and I think she does, she says she does, but it still drives me crazy."

"Whether or not she likes you, Don, or whether or not she loves you?"

"Yeah, that too. Whether or not she loves me."

Diane sat there and made listening noises the whole time I was talking, and when I told her how I will go days without eat-ing, she looked at me and sighed and ooohed and was definitely letting me know that this behavior was neither normal nor healthy. I think I could have told her that Elvis Presley was alive and living in my closet, and she would have been less surprised.

When you are a writer and a speaker, sometimes people think you have your crap together.

"You seem so normal, Don. You have a company and are a writer and all." Diane looked at me, bewildered.

"Yeah. But there is something wrong with me, isn't there?"

I was half hoping she would say no. I was hoping she would explain that everybody is nuts when they get into a relationship, but then it turns euphoric shortly after marriage and sex. But she didn't.

"Well, Don, there is. There is something wrong with you."

"Oh, man," I said. "I just knew it. I just knew I was a wacko." I thought about that movie *A Beautiful Mind* and wondered whether any of my housemates existed or whether those guys who kept following me were in the FBI.

Diane noted the concern on my face and responded, smiling and kind. "It's not that bad, Don. Don't worry. It's just that for some reason, you are letting this girl name you."

"What do you mean, name me?"

"Well, you are letting her decide your value, you know. Your value has to come from God. And God wants you to receive His love and to love yourself too."

And what she was saying was true. I knew it was true. I could feel that it was true. But it also felt wrong. I mean, it felt like it was an arrogant thing to do, to love myself, to receive love. I knew that all the kicking myself around, all the hating myself, was not coming from God, that those voices were not God whispering in my ear, but it felt like I had to listen to them; it felt like I had to believe the voices were telling the truth.

"God loves you, Don." Diane looked at me with a little moisture in her eyes. I felt like Matt Damon in that scene in *Good Will Hunting* where Robin Williams keeps saying, "It's not your fault, it's not your fault," and Matt Damon just freaks out and collapses into Robin Williams's arms and secures an Academy Award for both of them. I thought about acting out that scene with Diane, but it didn't feel right so I let it go.

"Yeah, I know," I told her. "I know God loves me." And I did know, I just didn't believe. It was such crap, such psychobabble. I had heard it before, but hearing that stuff didn't silence the voices. Still, there was something in Diane's motherly eyes that said it was true and I needed that; I needed to believe it was true. I needed something to tell the voices when they started chanting at me.

Diane and I talked for another half hour, and she oooohed and sighed and made me feel listened to. She was wonderful, and I never once felt stupid or weak for talking to her. I just felt honest and real and relieved. She said she would get me some literature and that she wanted to get together again soon. She said she would pray for me.

When she left, I decided to start praying about all of this too. I couldn't believe I hadn't prayed about it before. It's just that it never seemed like a spiritual problem. I prayed and asked God to help me figure out what was wrong with me.

Things got worse with the girl. We would spend hours on the phone working through the math of our relationship, but nothing added up, which I received as only a sign of my incompetence, and this made me more sad than before.

Then she did it; she decided we didn't need to be in touch anymore. She broke it off. She sent me a letter saying that I didn't love myself and could not receive love from her. There was nothing she could do about it, and it was killing her. I wandered around the house for an hour just looking at the blank walls, making coffee or cleaning the bathroom, not sure when my body was going to explode in sobs and tears. I was scrubbing the toilet when the voices began. I'd listened to them so often before, but on this day they were shouting. They were telling me that I was as disgusting as the urine on the wall around the toilet.

And then the sentiment occurred. I am certain it was the voice of God because it was accompanied by such a strong epiphany like a movement in a symphony or something. The sentiment was simple: *Love your neighbor as yourself.*

And I thought about that for a second and wondered why God would put that phrase so strongly in my mind. I thought about our neighbor Mark, who is tall and skinny and gay, and I wondered whether God was telling me I was gay, which was odd because I had never felt gay, but then it hit me that God was not telling me I was gay. He was saying I would never talk to my neighbor the way I talked to myself, and that somehow I had come to believe it was wrong to kick other people around but it was okay to do it to myself. It was as if God had put me in a plane and flown me over myself so I could see how I was connected, all the neighborhoods that were falling apart because I would not let myself receive love from myself, from others, or from God. And I wouldn't receive love because it felt so wrong. It didn't feel humble, and I knew I was supposed to be humble. But that was all crap, and it didn't make any sense. If it is wrong for me to receive love, then it is also wrong for me to give it because by giving it I am causing somebody else to receive it, which I had presupposed was the wrong thing to do. So I stopped. And I mean that. I stopped hating myself. It no longer felt right. It wasn't manly or healthy, and I cut it out. That was about a year ago, and since then I have been relatively happy. I am not kidding. I don't sit around and talk bad about myself anymore.

The girl and I got back together, and she could sense the difference in me, and she liked it, and I felt that I was operating a completely new machine. I couldn't believe how beautiful it was to receive love, to have the authority to love myself, to feel that it was right to love myself. When my girlfriend told me how she felt, I was able to receive it, and we had this normal relationship that in the end didn't work because we realized we weren't for each other. When we finally closed it out, it didn't hurt because I trusted that God had something else for me, and if He didn't, it didn't mean He didn't love me. From that point on, the point in the bathroom, I had confidence. Odd but true.

○   ○   ○

And so I have come to understand that strength, inner strength, comes from receiving love as much as it comes from giving it. I think apart from the idea that I am a sinner and God forgives me, this is the greatest lesson I have ever learned. When you get it, it changes you. My friend Julie from Seattle told me that the main prayer she prays for her husband is that he will be able to receive love. And this is the prayer I pray for all my friends because it is the key to happiness. God's love will never change us if we don't accept it.

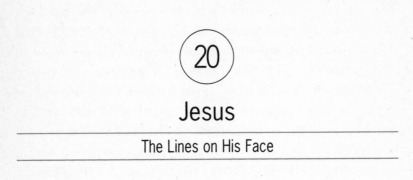

Jesus

The Lines on His Face

A GUY I KNOW NAMED ALAN WENT AROUND THE country asking ministry leaders questions. He went to successful churches and asked the pastors what they were doing, why what they were doing was working. It sounded very boring except for one visit he made to a man named Bill Bright, the president of a big ministry. Alan said he was a big man, full of life, who listened without shifting his eyes. Alan asked a few questions. I don't know what they were, but as a final question he asked Dr. Bright what Jesus meant to him. Alan said Dr. Bright could not answer the question. He said Dr. Bright just started to cry. He sat there in his big chair behind his big desk and wept.

When Alan told that story I wondered what it was like to love Jesus that way. I wondered, quite honestly, if that Bill Bright guy was just nuts or if he really knew Jesus in a personal way, so well that he would cry at the very mention of His name. I knew then that I would like to know Jesus like that, with my heart, not just my head. I felt like that would be the key to something.

o   o   o

I was watching one of those news shows on television several months ago about a woman whose son was on death row. He had killed a man and buried him in the woods. The television show followed the woman around during her son's last few days. The cameras were there for the last visit when the son, a young black man, sat across from his mother in the prison visiting room, and the mother had tears in her eyes and was trying so very hard to disguise the fear and regret and confusion and panic. I sat on the couch uncomfortably, and I wanted to jump through the screen and stop it all. I remember saying to myself, I hate this, but I kept watching. And there was a little girl there, the man's tiny sister, and she was sitting on his lap, and she didn't know he was going to die, but he was saying to be good and to do homework and don't tell any lies and obey her mama. Then the television showed the mother in her apartment a couple of days later, a sort of run-down hotel room in the ghetto, in the projects, and they didn't narrate anything, they just let the cameras roll as the woman paced up and down in front of the bed. The kids, the three beautiful children, ran in and out the open door, in and out of the heat where there was some sunset light happening. And the phone rang, and the woman went over and sat on the side of the bed and picked up the phone. She held it kind of shakily and listened without saying anything. She just said yes, in sort of a gut whisper, and then she put the phone back down, but it didn't hang up right. She fell to her knees and then got up and screamed and shook her fists at the ceiling. She turned and ran out the door, into the courtyard of this run-down apartment complex, and as the camera pulled to look out the open door they showed this large black woman collapse to the ground screaming into the dirt and pounding her fist.

I thought of that scene much later when my friend Julie and I were driving down from Yosemite listening to Patty Griffin sing

"Mary" on the CD player. In the song, Patty talks about Mary, the mother of Jesus, and what it must have been like the day her son was killed. She paints this painful picture of Mary inside her house, cleaning, and as the song played I imagined Mary washing down the counters and sweeping the floors, frantically, trying not to think about what they had done to her Son that morning. And I imagined Mary falling down outside her door on her hands and knees and beating her fists into the dirt and screaming at God.

Julie and I drove down from Glacier Point, and even though it was cold we turned on the heat and rolled down the windows so we could see the stars through the trees. We kept hitting repeat on the CD player and ended up listening to Patty Griffin sing about Mary more than forty consecutive times. I kept imagining Jesus in my mind like a real person, sometimes out in the wilderness like Yosemite Valley, sometimes by a fire talking with His friends, sometimes thinking about His mother, always missing His Father.

Rick leads a small group for people who do not believe in Jesus but have questions about Him. One of the people in the small group asked Rick what he thought Jesus looked like; did He look like the pictures on the walls of churches? Rick said he didn't know. One of the other people in the group spoke up very cautiously and said she thought perhaps he looked like Osama Bin Laden. Rick said this is probably very close to the truth.

Sometimes I picture this Osama Bin Laden–looking Jesus talking with His friends around a fire, except He is not rambling about anything, He is really listening, not so much pushing an agenda but being kind and understanding and speaking some truth and encouragement into their lives. Helping them believe in the mission they feel inside themselves, the mission that surrounded Jesus and the crazy life they had embraced.

I remember the first time I had feelings for Jesus. It wasn't very long ago. I had gone to a conference on the coast with some Reed students, and a man spoke who was a professor at a local Bible college. He spoke mostly about the Bible, about how we should read the Bible. He was convincing. He seemed to have an emotional relationship with the Book, the way I think about *Catcher in the Rye*. This man who was speaking reads through the Bible three times each year. I had never read through the Bible at all. I had read a lot of it but not all of it, and mostly I read it because I felt that I had to; it was healthy or something. The speaker guy asked us to go outside and find a quiet place and get reacquainted with the Book, hold it in our hands and let our eyes feel down the pages. I went out on the steps outside the rest room and opened my Bible to the book of James.

Years ago I had a crush on a girl, and I prayed about it and that night read through James, and because it is a book about faith and belief I felt like God was saying that if I had faith she would marry me. So I was very excited about this and lost a lot of weight, but the girl gave her virginity to a jerk from our youth group, and they are married now. I didn't care, honestly. I didn't love her that much. I only say that because the book of James, in my Bible, is highlighted in ten colors and underlined all over the place, and it looks blood raw, and the yellow pages remind me of a day when I believed so faithfully in God, so beautifully in God. I read a little, maybe a few pages, then shut the book, very tired and confused. But when we got back from the conference, I felt like my Bible was calling me. I felt this promise that if I read it, if I just read it like a book, cover to cover, it wouldn't change me into an idiot, it wouldn't change me into a clone of Pat Buchanan, and that was honestly the thing I was worried about with the Bible. If I read it, it would make me simple in my thinking. So I started in Matthew,

which is one of the Gospels about Jesus. And I read through
Matthew and Mark, then Luke and John. I read those books in a
week or so, and Jesus was very confusing, and I didn't know if I
liked Him very much, and I was certainly tired of Him by the second day. By the time I got to the end of Luke, to the part where
they were going to kill Him again, where they were going to
stretch Him out on a cross, something shifted within me. I
remember it was cold outside, crisp, and the leaves in the trees of
the park across the street were getting tired and dry. And I remember sitting at my desk, and I don't know what it was that I read or
what Jesus was doing in the book, but I felt a love for Him rush
through me, through my back and into my chest. I started crying,
too, like that guy Bill Bright.

I remember thinking that I would follow Jesus anywhere, that
it didn't matter what He asked me to do. He could be mean to
me; it didn't matter, I loved Him, and I was going to follow Him.

I think the most important thing that happens within
Christian spirituality is when a person falls in love with Jesus.

Sometimes when I go forward at church to take Communion,
to take the bread and dip it in the wine, the thought of Jesus
comes to me, the red of His blood or the smell of His humanity,
and I eat the bread and I wonder at the mystery of what I am
doing, that somehow I am one with Christ, that I get my very
life from Him, my spiritual life comes from His working inside
me, being inside me.

I know our culture will sometimes understand a love for Jesus
as weakness. There is this lie floating around that says I am supposed to be able to do life alone, without any help, without stopping to worship something bigger than myself. But I actually
believe there is something bigger than me, and I need for there
to be something bigger than me. I need someone to put awe
inside me; I need to come second to someone who has everything figured out.

○   ○   ○

All great characters in stories are the ones who give their lives to something bigger than themselves. And in all of the stories I don't find anyone more noble than Jesus. He gave His life for me, in obedience to His Father. I truly love Him for it. I feel that, and so does Laura and Penny and Rick and Tony the Beat Poet. I think the difference in my life came when I realized, after reading those Gospels, that Jesus didn't just love me out of principle; He didn't just love me because it was the right thing to do. Rather, there was something inside me that caused Him to love me. I think I realized that if I walked up to His campfire, He would ask me to sit down, and He would ask me my story. He would take the time to listen to my ramblings or my anger until I could calm down, and then He would look me directly in the eye, and He would speak to me; He would tell me the truth, and I would sense in his voice and in the lines on His face that he liked me. He would rebuke me, too, and he would tell me that I have prejudices against very religious people and that I need to deal with that; He would tell me that there are poor people in the world and I need to feed them and that somehow this will make me more happy. I think He would tell me what my gifts are and why I have them, and He would give me ideas on how to use them. I think He would explain to me why my father left, and He would point out very clearly all the ways God has taken care of me through the years, all the stuff God protected me from.

○   ○   ○

After I got Laura's e-mail in which she told me she had become a Christian, I just about lost it with excitement. I felt like a South African the day they let Mandela out of prison. I called her and asked her to coffee at Palio. I picked her up in Eliot Circle at Reed, and she was smiling and full of energy. She said we had much to talk about, very much to talk about. At Palio, we sat in the booth at the back, and even though Laura had been my close friend, I felt like I had never met this woman. She squirmed in her seat as she talked with confidence about her love for Jesus. I sat there amazed because it is true. People do come to know Jesus. This crazy thing really happens. It isn't just me.

o   o   o

I was watching BET one night, and they were interviewing a man about jazz music. He said jazz music was invented by the first generation out of slavery. I thought that was beautiful because, while it is music, it is very hard to put on paper; it is so much more a language of the soul. It is as if the soul is saying something, something about freedom. I think Christian spirituality is like jazz music. I think loving Jesus is something you feel. I think it is something very difficult to get on paper. But it is no less real, no less meaningful, no less beautiful.

The first generation out of slavery invented jazz music. It is a music birthed out of freedom. And that is the closest thing I know to Christian spirituality. A music birthed out of freedom. Everybody sings their song the way they feel it, everybody closes their eyes and lifts up their hands.

o   o   o

I want Jesus to happen to you the way He happened to Laura at Reed, the way He happened to Penny in France, the way He happened to me in Texas. I want you to know Jesus too. This book is about the songs my friends and I are singing. This is what

God is doing in our lives. But what song will you sing when your soul gets set free? I think it will be something true and beautiful. If you haven't done it in a while, pray and talk to Jesus. Ask Him to become real to you. Ask Him to forgive you of self-addiction, ask Him to put a song in your heart. I can't think of anything better that could happen to you than this. Much love to you and thanks for listening to us sing.

Acknowledgments

THANK YOU, KATHY HELMERS, FOR YOUR ENCOURAGEMENT and help in getting this book to a publisher, and to Lee and Alice and the rest of the crew at Alive for their generous hearts and diligent work. Much gratitude to the people at Thomas Nelson for rolling the dice; those people are Brian, Jonathan, Kyle, Ashley, Pamela, Laurie, Belinda, Blythe, Amy, Danielle, Kathleen, Carol, Andrea, Paula, Tina, Louetta, Kristen, Jenny, Deonne, and interns Stacey and Sarah. And thanks to the rest of that great crew at Thomas Nelson including the huge sales staff on the road who don't get thanked enough. Also thanks to media trainer Joel Roberts.

My friends gave their lives to me and then kindly let me write about our relationships, which was something vulnerable and giving, so thanks to Tony, Penny, Laura, Andrew the Protester, Rick, Mark the Cussing Pastor, Les, the Tunnell family, Wes and Maja Bjur, Paul and Danielle, Mike, Josh, Jeremy, Heather, Kurt, Curtis, Mitch, Simon, Trevor, Michael, Stacy, Diane, Wes, Grant, Julie the Canadian, Matt and Julie Canlis, Rachel Clifton for being the second mom to so many of us, the guys at Graceland, and the guys at Testosterhome too. Also, the people I love at Imago-Dei Community and my family.

Thanks Josh, Gregg, and Sono for giving me a start. And to John and Terri MacMurray, who were like family away from family. Thanks Wes and Maja for letting me live in your attic for so long and as always for your love and kindness.

Thanks, Peter Jenkins, for your drawings, and Steve Harmon, for author shots, video stuff, and encouragement. Thanks, David Allen, for your work on cover comps. I owe you one. Thanks to Tony's grad class at Multnomah for reading the manuscript and giving encouragement; those folks are Shemaiah, Lindsey, Toby, Steve, and Nicole. Thanks to James Prior for bringing me so often to San Fran and for your friendship. This book was written at Common Ground, Palio, Horse Brass Pub, the downtown coffee shops including Seattle's Best, Vista Springs, and a few others I can't remember, but thanks to these fine establishments for their good coffee and beer. Thanks to tri-met for getting me around. "How we get there matters!" While I wrote I listened to Patty Griffin, the Pogues, Bruce Springsteen, Eliot Smith, Lyle, Whiskeytown, Phil Roy, Big Head Todd and the Monsters, the Jayhawks, P.O.D., Tori Amos, Steve Earle, Bob Schneider, Moby, the Beatles, and my current favorite, Wilco (*Yankee Hotel Foxtrot* had just come out when I started the project, and we were all amazed and happy), so strange thanks to the makers of the sound track.

Thank you for reading this book. It means a great deal to me that you would take the time. I hope we get to meet some day soon.

Donald Miller has written for *Believe Magazine, HM Magazine, Killing the Buddha,* and many other publications. He is a frequent speaker on issues relating to Christian spirituality, literature, and culture. He lives in Portland, Oregon.

For information about Donald Miller, or to book him for speaking engagements, please visit:

www.bluelikejazz.com

To use Don Rabbit and Don Astronaut as illustrations, download the images at:

www.bluelikejazz.com

For more information on Don's writing, as well as other thought-provoking authors' works, visit:

www.BurnsideWritersCollective.com

Also Available from
Donald Miller

Donald Miller's *Through Painted Deserts* chronicles free spirits Don and Paul as they set off on an adventure-filled road trip in search of deeper meaning, beauty, and an explanation for life. Along the way, everything from the nature of friendship to the reason for pain is discussed as these two friends learn unexpected lessons about themselves, each other, and even God.

ISBN 0-7852-0982-4

In *Searching for God Knows What,* Donald Miller shows readers how most people believe millions of gospels or systems for fixing their brokenness, and why all of them are fruitless except the amazing gospel of Jesus. In this provocative and funny book, Miller shows that the greatest desire of every person is that of redemption and how it can only be truly found through this gospel.

ISBN 0-7852-6371-3